KU-770-258

BR STEAM MOTIVE POWER DEPOTS

BR STEAM MOTIVE POWER DEPOTS

ScR

Paul Bolger

Inverness shed as viewed from the top of the coaling tower. When built it was intended that the depot would eventually form a complete circle and the arched water tower act as an entrance. P. L. Melvill

LONDON

IAN ALLAN LTD

First published 1983

ISBN 0 7110 1248 2

All rights reserved. No part of this book may be reproduced or transmitted in any form or by any means, electronic or mechanical, including photo-copying, recording or by any information storage and retrieval system, without permission from the Publisher in writing.

© Paul Bolger, 1983

Published by Ian Allan Ltd, Shepperton, Surrey; and printed by Ian Allan Printing Ltd at their works at Coombelands in Runnymede, England

Preface

The purpose of this book is to assist the average enthusiast be he modeller, relic collector or historian, with his search for information on Motive Power Depots — the home of the steam locomotive.

Many devotees will recall the experience of touring such an establishment; the hiss of steam, the clank of engine movements and the sight of smoke suspended from the ceilings above the many varieties of engine in different stages of repair.

The sight of a fully serviced locomotive simmering outside the depot on a crisp bright morning is a memory I shall never forget. I hope that the following pages aid the reminiscences of those fortunate enough to have lived during the steam age.

This book is dedicated to George Ellis, a native Scot and informative and valued friend to many enthusiasts, myself included.

Paul Bolger

Introduction

For reasons of parity with the previous volumes — *BR Steam Motive Power Depots LMR and ER* (both by Ian Allan Ltd) — the depots covered by this work have been restricted to those which possessed a code, as these were the most visited and of greater importance to the railway network.

In all, 44 depots are outlined and because of the lesser numbers of sheds by comparison with the LMR volume, a minimum of two views per shed have been included with some having as many as five. For continuity of the text the codes used as headings are c1950.

Acknowledgements

This book has been made possible with the invaluable help of the following people and organisations: Director of Public Affairs at British Rail Glasgow; Mr Winch and Mr Fairclough of the Cambridge University Library; Miss S. Percy of the Ordnance Survey; Mr C. Turner of Photomatic; Mr G. M. Kitchenside of Locomotive & General Railway Photographs and Mr Rhodes of Real Photos.

In addition, special thanks are extended to the following: D. A. Anderson, D. Birch, H. I. Cameron, D. Carville, H. C. Casserley, F. Dean, D. J. Dippie, D. R. Easton, A. G. Ellis, K. Fairey, P. Foster, B. K. B. Green, B. Hilton, C. Lofthus, F. Lyon, K. K. Mackay, D. Mackinnon, A. W. Martin, P. L. Melvill, G. W. Morrison, P. R. Parham, K. R. Pirt, M. Pope, W. Potter, N. E. Preedy, G. Reeve, D. Rendell, S. Rickard, G. W. Sharpe, R. E. B. Siviter, J. L. Stevenson, W. T. Stubbs, D. B. Swale, R. E. Vincent and T. Wright.

In the course of preparation the following publications were of major importance as reference and consultative material: *The Railway Observer* (Volumes 18-38); *The Railway Magazine* (Volumes 94-114); the *Railway World* (Volumes 19-29); *Trains Illustrated* and *Modern Railways* (Volumes 3-21).

Notes about Contents

The ex-North British shed at Carlisle Canal has been catered for in the LMR volume (as 12B) as it both started and ended its BR existence under the control of that region. The Scottish sector of the ex-LMS sheds (Groups 27A to 32C) have all been included with their revised BR Scottish Region codes except 29C Dundee West. This depot never received a new code and survived only as a sub-shed in the Scottish Region. It has, however, been accommodated in the London Midland volume as 29C on the basis that it would have retained its coded status until 1949 when its fate was decided.

Many points can be raised in qualifying the inclusion or exclusion of certain depots, but it must be remembered that strict compliance with the coding system would have resulted in severe duplication of the contents of this and the LMR volume. A balance has, therefore, been struck in an attempt to combat the effects of BR's failure to issue each region with its codes in January 1948. It is hoped the resulting regional 'limbo' where it occurs will not hinder your enjoyment of the book.

Pre-Grouping Origins

Although, primarily, not relevant to the period covered, an indication of the vintage of the shed is given by the inclusion of the company of ownership prior to 1923. This is not necessarily the company which commissioned the building, as many smaller installations were absorbed into the larger companies by the takeover or amalgamation of district railways.

Gazetteer References

These numbers refer to the page and square within the Ian Allan Pre-Grouping Atlas which pinpoint the subject's national location.

Closing Dates

The dates given indicate the closure of the depot to steam engines only. However, in some cases the date would have been the same for diesels where the building closed completely, either as a result of its dilapidated condition or the effects of the 'Beeching' cuts.

Shed Codes

The Scottish Region was not issued with shed codes at the outset of nationalisation in 1948 owing to BR's indecision over districts. In 1949 it was allocated ex-LMS type codes commencing with 60A.

Allocations

Where the depot's lifetime allows, three separate allocations, of steam locomotives only, are listed from the years 1950, 1959 and 1965. These lists are accurate to August 1950, February 1959 and April 1965.

Plans

All the plans have been based upon the Ordnance Survey County Series and National Grid maps from various years with the exception of the undermentioned. Reproduction is by permission of the Controller of Her Majesty's Stationery Office, Crown Copyright Reserved.
60B, 60C, 60E, 68A.

Photographs

All except nine of the 133 illustrations have been restricted to the period 1948/67. The greater majority of the views are hitherto unpublished and represent many years of search.

60A INVERNESS

Pre-Grouping Origin: Highland Railway
Gazetteer Ref: 36 E5
Closed: 1962
Shed-Codes: 32A (1948 to 1949)
60A (1949 to 1962)
Allocations: 1950

A westerly view of Inverness in 1957 taken from an elevated position in the nearby Millburn Road. The town can be seen in the background.
J. L. Stevenson

Class 5MT 4-6-0

44783	44991	45120	45179	45461
44784	44992	45122	45192	45476
44785	45012	45123	45319	45477
44788	45053	45124	45320	45478
44789	45066	45136	45360	45479
44798	45090	45138	45361	
44799	45098	45160	45453	

Class 3P 4-4-0

54439	54470	54472	54487	54496
54463	54471	54484	54491	

Class 2P 0-4-4T
55160   55199

Class OF 0-4-0ST
56011   56038

Class 3F 0-6-0T

56262	56291	56293	56299	56341

Class 3F 0-6-0

57591	57597	57634	57642

Class 4F 4-6-0

57951	57954	57955	57956

Class Y9 0-4-0ST
68108

Total 60

Allocations: 1959

Class 5 4-6-0

44718	44785	45066	45192	45461
44719	44788	45090	45319	45476
44722	44789	45098	45320	45477
44723	44798	45117	45360	45478
44724	44799	45123	45361	45479
44783	44991	45124	45453	
44784	44992	45179	45460	

Class 3P 4-4-0

54463	54487	54493	54496

Looking from the turntable to the shed-yard in 1960 with the threat of dieselisation drawing nearer.
K. Fairey

Pure nostalgia. Inverness shed in 1913 with many pre-grouping refinements in evidence; free-standing smoke stacks, shed doors and a covered turntable. LGRP courtesy David & Charles

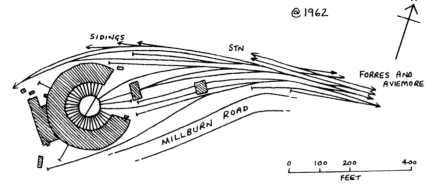

@ 1962

N

SIDINGS

STN

FORRES AND
AVIEMORE

MILLBURN ROAD

0   100   200   400
FEET

Class 2P 0-4-4T
55198   55216   55227
55199   55226   55236

Class OF 0-4-0ST
56038

Class 3F 0-6-0T
56300   56305   56341

Class 3F 0-6-0
57575   57594   57661

Total 50

The four Class 4F 4-6-0 engines allocated to Inverness in 1950 were the only survivors of the ex-Highland Railway 'Clan Goods' class and were all withdrawn by 1953. Between April and June 1962, most of the steam allocation was withdrawn or transferred to the Glasgow area but the final few stored engines went to Perth (63A) in August of the same year.

The view of Inverness which was obtained when passing by train. K. Fairey

60B AVIEMORE

Pre-Grouping Origin: Highland Railway
Gazetteer Ref: 36 F3
Closed: 1962
Shed-Codes: 32B (1948 to 1949)
60B (1949 to 1962)
Allocations: 1950

Class 5MT 4-6-0
45018

Class 3P 4-4-0
54455   54466   54488   54493

*Looking north-east to Aviemore in 1953 with
No 62277 Gordon Highlander (61C) facing the
camera. This loco was withdrawn in June 1958 and
restored to its original livery as GNSR No 49. On the
left of the view, Class 2P 0-4-4T No 55174, an
Aviemore loco, can just be seen.* J. L. Stevenson

Class 2P 0-4-4T
55174

Class 3F 0-6-0
57586

Total 7

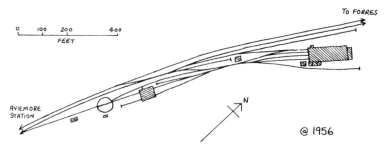

Another view of Aviemore, this time in 1954 with a 'Black Five' and Class 3MT 2-6-2T on parade. Photomatic

Allocations: 1959

Class 4 2-6-4T
42269

Class 5 4-6-0
45136

Class 3P 4-4-0
54466   54482   54484   54488

Class 2P 0-4-4T
55173

Class 3F 0-6-0
57586   57591   57597   57632

Class 2 2-6-0
78052

Total 12

The last engine was transferred away in July 1962.

60C HELMSDALE

Pre-Grouping Origin: Highland Railway
Gazetteer Ref: 38 F4
Closed: 1962
Shed-Code: 60C (1949 to 1962)
Allocations: 1950

Helmsdale in 1953 looking south-east to the station and depot. The shed roof was in bad need of repair by this time. B. Hilton

Class 3P 4-4-0
54480   54495

Class 1P 0-4-4T
55051   55053

Class 3F 0-6-0
57587

Total 5

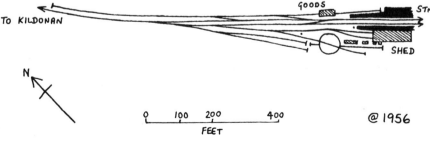

Allocations: 1959

Class 16xx 0-6-0PT
1646   1649

Class 3P 4-4-0
54470   54480   54495

Class 3F 0-6-0
57587

Total 6

A 1959 view of the shed with 'Black Five' No 44718 (60A) and 16xx 0-6-0PT No 1646 at rest outside. The latter engine arrived in 1957 for work on the Dornoch Branch (see shed-notes). N. E. Preedy

Ex-Western Region locos, Nos 1646 and 1649 arrived at Helmsdale in 1957 and 1958 respectively for 'Push-Pull' employment on the Dornoch branch.

60D WICK

Pre-Grouping Origin: Highland Railway
Gazetteer Ref: 38 D2
Closed: 1962
Shed-Code: 60D (1949 to 1962)
Allocations: 1950

An easterly view of Wick shed in 1949.
J. L. Stevenson

'Ben' Class 2P 4-4-0
54398 *Ben Alder*
54399 *Ben Wyvis*
54404 *Ben Clebrig*

Class 3P 4-4-0
54445

Class 3F 0-6-0
57585

Total 5

Wick a decade later with two Inverness 'Black Fives' on shed. Note that their numbers are consecutive left to right; Nos 44783 and 44784. Photomatic

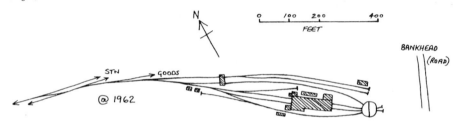

Allocations: 1959

Class 3 2-6-2T
40150

Class 3P 4-4-0
54491

Class 3F 0-6-0
57585

Total 3

As will be seen the last three 'Ben' class engines (ex-HR) were allocated here in 1950. The sole survivor 54398 'Ben Alder' was withdrawn a few years later for eventual preservation in its original livery as Highland Railway No 2.

With the exception of its sub-shed Thurso, Wick was the most northerly motive power depot in the British Isles. Steam closure came in July 1962 when much of the ex-Highland system was dieselised.

Wick shed in 1949 as viewed from the turntable. Inside the shed is Class 2P 4-4-0 No 54404 Ben Clebrig *(60D).* B. K. B. Green

60E FORRES

Pre-Grouping Origin: Highland Railway
Gazetteer Ref: 36 D3
Closed: 1959
Shed-Codes: 32C (1948 to 1949)
60E (1949 to 1959)
Allocations: 1950

Class 3P 4-4-0
54473   54481   54482

Class 3F 0-6-0T
56301

Class 3F 0-6-0
57620

Total 5

*Forres shed in 1954 with Class 3P 4-4-0 No 54482
(60E) framed at the entrance.* J. L. Stevenson

Allocations: 1959

Class 3P 4-4-0
54471   54472   54473

Class 2P 0-4-4T
55269

Class 3F 0-6-0T
56291

Class 3F 0-6-0
57620

Total 6

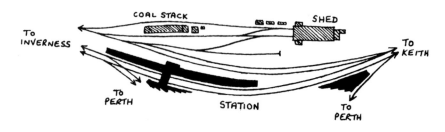

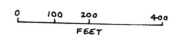

@ 1956

0   100   200   400

FEET

N

12

Forres was the first of the main ex-Highland depots to close to steam. In May 1959 its last four engines (Nos 54471/2, 55269, 57620) were transferred to Inverness (60A), St Rollox (65B) and Polmadie (66A).

Another view in the same year looking north-east. The shed's sole '3F' 0-6-0, No 57620 is outside awaiting its next turn of duty. Photomatic

61A KITTYBREWSTER

Pre-Grouping Origin: Great North of Scotland Railway
Gazetteer Ref: 37 F4
Closed: 1961
Shed-Code: 61A (1949 to 1961)
Allocations: 1950

Class 2P 4-4-0

40603	40622	40650

Class B1 4-6-0

61134	61324	61348	61351	61401
61307	61343	61349	61352	61404
61323	61345	61350	61400	

Class B12 4-6-0

61505	61511	61524	61532	61552
61507	61513	61526	61539	61560
61508	61521	61528	61543	61563

Class D41 4-4-0

62225	62229	62232
62228	62230	62241

Class D40 4-4-0

62260	62265	62270
62261	62268	62272

62273 *George Davidson*
62274 *Benachie*
62275 *Sir David Stewart*
62276 *Andrew Bain*
62277 *Gordon Highlander*
62278 *Hatton Castle*
62279 *Glen Grant*

Looking across the turntable at Kittybrewster towards the shed yard and coaling plant in 1954. Photomatic

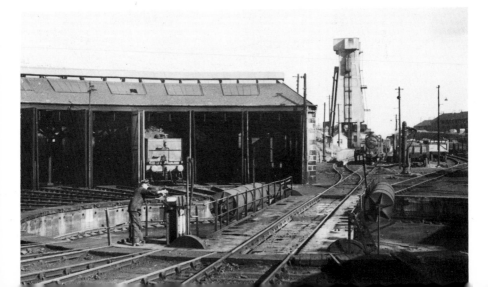

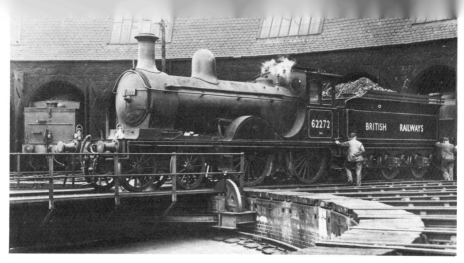

Class J36 0-6-0
65247

Class F4 2-4-2T
67151   67157   67164

Class G5 0-4-4T
67287   67327

Class VI 2-6-2T
67667   67671

Classes Z4 & Z5* 0-4-2T
68190   68191   68192*   68193*

Class J72 0-6-0T
68700   68717   68749
68710   68719   68750

Class N14 0-6-2T
69125

Total 70

Class D40 4-4-0 No 62272 assisting with shunting movements at Kittybrewster in 1950.   A. G. Ellis

Allocations: 1959

Class 2P 4-4-0
40603   40604   40648   40650   40663

Class 2 2-6-0
46460

Class BI 4-6-0
61242 *Alexander Reith Gray*
61294   61345   61347   61352
61324   61346   61350   61400

Looking west across the track radii in 1954 clearly showing the differing styles of building prevelant at the depot. This type of contrast was not always the product of shed expansion as fires and general dilapidation were quite often the root cause of a rebuilding programme.   J. L. Stevenson

Class B12 4-6-0 No 61536 on the turntable at Kittybrewster in 1949.   W. Potter

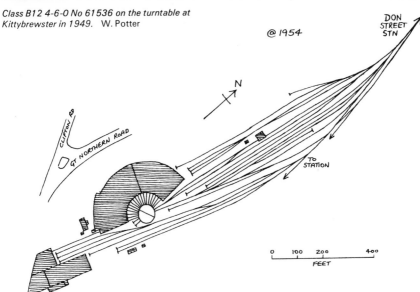

@ 1954

DON
STREET
STN

N

CLIFTON RD

GT NORTHERN ROAD

TO
STATION

0   100   200   400
FEET

Class K2 2-6-0					Class J72 0-6-0T			
61741					68717	68719	68749	68750
61790 *Loch Lomond*								

Class D34 4-4-0
62479 *Glen Sheil*
62480 *Glen Fruin*
62482 *Glen Mamie*
62489 *Glen Dessary*
62493 *Glen Gloy*
62497 *Glen Mallie*
62498 *Glen Moidart*

Class J36 0-6-0

65221	65227	65251	65297	65303

Classes Z4 & Z5* 0-4-2T
68190   65192*

Class N15 0-6-2T
69180

Class 4 2-6-0
76104   76108

Class 2 2-6-0
78045

Class 4 2-6-4T

80004	80021	80111	80114
80005	80028	80112	80115
80020	80029	80113	

Total 50

15

Kittybrewster shed possessed a highly mixed bag of motive power throughout its BR existence. The 1950 allocation portrays locomotives which first saw the light of day on Great Eastern metals. Other pre-grouping companies represented (apart from the GNOSR) were the North British and North Eastern.

At closure in August 1961 the last few locomotives transferred to Ferryhill (61B). Dieselisation was more or less complete on the ex-GNOSR by September of the same year. The roof of the larger section of the shed was demolished in 1956.

61B FERRYHILL

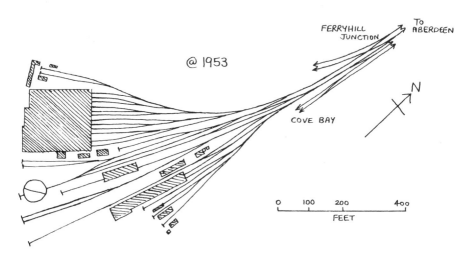

@ 1953

FERRYHILL JUNCTION

To ABERDEEN

COVE BAY

N

0   100   200   400
FEET

Pre-Grouping Origin: Caledonian and North British Joint Railways*
Gazetteer Ref: 37 G4
Closed: 1967
Shed-Codes: 29B (1948 to 1949)
61B (1949 to 1967)
Allocations: 1950

Class 4P 4-4-0
41134   41176   41184

Class 3F 0-6-0T
56240   56251   56278   56326   56348

Class A2 4-6-2
60525 *A. H. Peppercorn*
60531 *Bahram*
60537 *Bachelors Button*

A south-westerly view of Ferryhill in 1957. Despite its 12 roads, the shed never really had a sizeable allocation in BR days and as such must have been one of the few depots, of this dimension, in the country capable of sheltering its complement of engines.   J. L. Stevenson

A post-grouping view of the joint depot with LMS and LNER types sharing the metals.
Ian Allan Library

Class V2 2-6-2
60819 60827 60898 60970
60822 60851 60919 60973
60824 60888 60955

Class B1 4-6-0
61132 61133

Class J39 0-6-0
64795 64975

Class J36 0-6-0
65213 65297

Class C15 4-4-2T
67455 67478

Class J69 0-6-0T
68568

Class N15 0-6-2T
69128 69129 69201

Class WD 2-8-0
90041 90121 90260
90097 90203 90455
                                    Total 40

Allocations: 1959

Class 2P 4-4-0
40617 40618

Class 5 4-6-0
44703 44794 45162 45167 45469

Class 3F 0-6-0T
56240 56278 56325 56326

Class A2 4-6-2
60525 *A. H. Peppercorn*
60531 *Bahram*
60532 *Blue Peter*

Class V2 2-6-2
60851 60898 60955 60972
60888 60919 60970 60973

Class J36 0-6-0
65305

Class N15 0-6-2T
69127 69128 69138 69224

Class WD 2-8-0
90041 90097 90455
                                    Total 30

Allocations: 1965

Class 5MT 4-6-0
44703 44794

Class A4 4-6-2
60004 *William Whitelaw*
60006 *Sir Ralph Wedgewood*
60007 *Sir Nigel Gresley*
60009 *Union of South Africa*
60010 *Dominion of Canada*
60019 *Bittern*
60026 *Miles Beevor*
60034 *Lord Faringdon*

Class 5MT 4-6-0
73008 73056

Class WD 2-8-0
90041 90596 90640
                                    Total 15

* Despite not having their own road to Aberdeen, the North British Railway obtained running powers over Caledonian metals from Kinnaber Junction to the city and with them a share of Ferryhill depot.

Ferryhill began acquiring the 'A4' Pacifics in 1962 and by 1965 possessed eight of the remaining 11 examples. The class became extinct in September 1966.

Closure came in March 1967 when the last few locos transferred to Dundee Tay Bridge (62B).

61C KEITH

Pre-Grouping Origin: Great North of Scotland Railway
Gazetteer Ref: 37 D1
Closed: 1961
Shed-Code: 61C (1949 to 1961)
Allocations: 1950

Keith shed in 1949 with three Class D40 4-4-0's and a 'B12' 4-6-0 occupying the four roads.
J. L. Stevenson

Class B1 4-6-0
61308	61346	61347	61353

Class B12 4-6-0
61501	61502	61503

Class D41 4-4-0
62227	62243	62248	62252
62231	62246	62249	62255
62242	62247	62251	62256

Class D40 4-4-0
62262	62264	62267	62269	62271

Class G5 0-4-4T
67292

Total 25

Allocations: 1959

Class 3 2-6-2T
40011

Class 2P 4-4-0
40600	40622

Class 2P 0-4-4T
55185	55221

Class 3F 0-6-0T
56348

Class 3F 0-6-0
57634

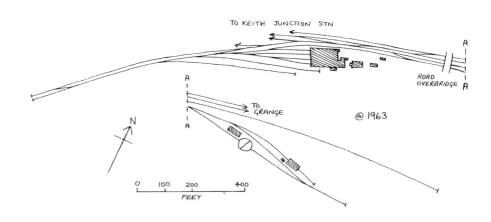

Class 3F 0-6-0 No 57591 at Keith in 1960.
Real Photos

Class K2 2-6-0
61755
61779
61782 *Loch Eil*
61783 *Loch Shiel*
61792

Class D34 4-4-0
62469 *Glen Douglas*

Class J36 0-6-0

65247	65267	65304	65310	65338

Class 2 2-6-0
78053   78054

Class 4 2-6-4T
80121   80122

Total 22

Keith shed lost its allocation in June 1961 and the remaining engines went to Ferryhill (61B), Dalry Road (64C), Bathgate (64F) and Corkerhill (67A). After years of virtual dereliction the shed underwent extensive rebuilding in 1953.

62A THORNTON

Pre-Grouping Origin: North British Railway
Gazetteer Ref: 30 A2
Closed: 1967
Shed Code: 62A (1949 to 1967)
Allocations: 1950

Class B1 4-6-0

61072	61118	61148
61103	61146	61262

Class D29 4-4-0
62410 *Ivanhoe*
62411 *Lady of Avenel*

A 1965 view of the eastern end of Thornton Junction shed with Classes J37 0-6-0 No 64569 and WD 2-8-0 No 90020, both 62A, facing the camera.
K. Fairey

Class B1 4-6-0 No 61133 (62A) is in the centre of this 1966 scene of the eastern end of the depot.
K. Fairey

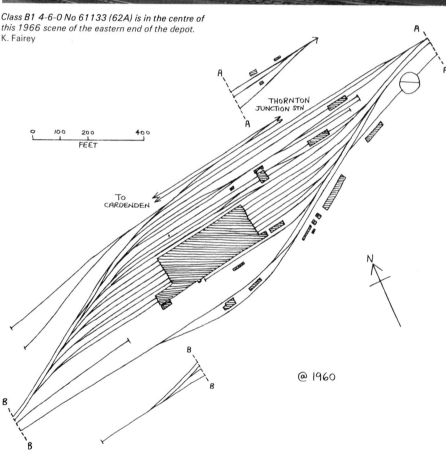

THORNTON
JUNCTION STN

0   100   200   400
FEET

To
CARDENDEN

N

@ 1960

Class D30 4-4-0
62418 *The Pirate*
62419 *Meg Dods*
62429 *The Abbot*
62430 *Jingling Geordie*
62431 *Kenilworth*
62442 *Simon Glover*

Class D34 4-4-0
62467 *Glenfinnan*
62468 *Glen Orchy*
62475 *Glen Beasdale*
62478 *Glen Quoich*
62492 *Glen Garvin*

Class D49 4-4-0
62704 *Stirlingshire*
62708 *Argyllshire*
62716 *Kincardineshire*
62717 *Banffshire*
62729 *Rutlandshire*

Class J35 0-6-0
64464	64477	64500	64521
64466	64488	64514	64522
64474	64495	64516	

Class J37 0-6-0
64546	64564	64597	64612	64629
64549	64565	64600	64616	64635
64550	64596	64602	64618	

Class J36 0-6-0
65218	65291	65345

Class J38 0-6-0
65901	65904	65910	65921	65932
65902	65907	65911	65925	
65903	65908	65913	65931	

Class C15 4-4-2T
67452	67476

Class J88 0-6-0T
68321	68323	68335	68341
68322	68332	68337	68353

Class J83 0-6-0T
68451	68456	68459
68453	68458	68467

Class J69 0-6-0T
68504	68535	68550	68555

Class N15 0-6-2T
69132	69153	69223
69150	69211	69224

Class WD 2-8-0
90004	90145	90282	90489	90614
90019	90168	90300	90498	90690
90049	90170	90319	90534	
90058	90177	90350	90539	
90128	90182	90472	90547	

Total 113

Inside Thornton shed in 1966 with Class J37 0-6-0 Nos 64570 and 64569 (both 62A) facing.
K. K. MacKay

Allocations: 1959

Class 2P 0-4-4T
55217

Class B1 4-6-0
61103	61134	61148	61330	61401
61118	61146	61262	61343	61403
61133	61147	61277	61358	

Class D30 4-4-0
62418 *The Pirate*

Class D34 4-4-0
62467 *Glenfinnan*
62475 *Glen Beasdale*
62478 *Glen Quoich*
62492 *Glen Garvin*

Class D11 4-4-0
62677 *Edie Ochiltree*

Class D49 4-4-0
62708 *Argyllshire*
62712 *Morayshire*
62716 *Kincardineshire*
62728 *Cheshire*
62729 *Rutlandshire*
62733 *Northumberland*
62744 *The Holderness*

Class J35 0-6-0
64466	64474	64488	64522

Class J37 0-6-0
64546	64564	64600	64618
64549	64565	64602	64629
64550	64596	64616	64635

Class J36 0-6-0
65218	65252	65345

Class J38 0-6-0
65900	65903	65907	65911	65925
65901	65904	65908	65913	65931
65902	65905	65910	65921	65932

This view of the western end of Thornton depicts Classes J38 0-6-0 No 65901 and B1 4-6-0 No 61343 (both 62A).   W. T. Stubbs

Class J88 0-6-0T

68332	68334	68335	69353

Class J83 0-6-0T

68453	68456	68458	68459

Class J72 0-6-0T

69012

Class N15 0-6-2T

69132	69143	69223

Class 4 2-6-0

76109	76110	76111

Class WD 2-8-0

90004	90117	90350	90534	90705
90019	90128	90441	90539	
90020	90168	90472	90614	
90058	90182	90513	90690	

Total 94

A pair of WD 2-8-0s Nos 90628 and 90441 (both 62A) simmering inside Thornton in 1965.   D. Birch

Allocations: 1965

Class B1 4-6-0

61103	61133	61261	61343
61132	61148	61330	

Class J37 0-6-0

64569	64588	64606	64625
64570	64595	64618	64632

Class J36 0-6-0

65345

Class J38 0-6-0

65901	65909	65914	65922
65905	65910	65915	65925
65907	65911	65916	65932

Class WD 2-8-0

90020	90168	90441	90468	90727
90117	90350	90444	90628	

Total 37

Thornton shed, sometimes known as Thornton Junction, lost its allocation in April 1967, but Class J36 0-6-0 No 65345 remained in store until June of the same year pending possible use in a film.

62B DUNDEE TAY BRIDGE

Looking north-east to Dundee Tay Bridge depot in 1959. W. T. Stubbs

Pre-Grouping Origin: North British Railway
Gazetteer Ref: 34 E4
Closed: 1967
Shed Code: 62B (1949 to 1967)
Allocations: 1950

Class 5MT 4-6-0
44954

Class 2MT 2-6-0
46463   46464

Class 2P 0-4-4T

55173	55192	55223	55227
55186	55217	55226	55231

Class 3F 0-6-0T
56323   56325

Class 3F 0-6-0
57568   57653

Class A2 4-6-2
60527 *Sun Chariot*
60528 *Tudor Minstrel*

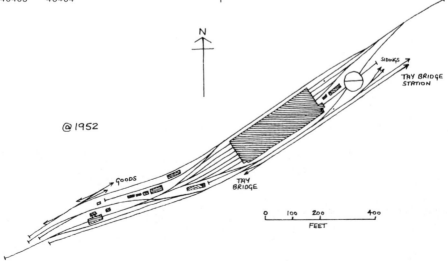

Towards the end of steam Dundee Tay Bridge possessed the last three remaining Class A2 Pacifics. All three are depicted here in 1966 (left to right), 60532 Blue Peter, *60528* Tudor Minstrel *and 60530* Sayajirao. M. Pope

Class V2 2-6-2

60804	60840	60920	60937	60969
60838	60844	60931	60958	60971

Class B1 4-6-0

61101	61147	61278	61293	61403
61102	61263	61292	61402	

Class D30 4-4-0
62427 *Dumbiedykes*
62434 *Kettledrummle*
62436 *Lord Glenvarloch*
62438 *Peter Poundtext*

Class D33 4-4-0
62457   62466

Class D34 4-4-0
62485 *Glen Murran*

Class D49 4-4-0
62713 *Aberdeenshire*
62718 *Kinross-shire*
62728 *Cheshire*

Class J35 0-6-0 No 64492 being turned at the north eastern end of Tay Bridge in 1954. Note that the table is the vacuum assisted type which enabled the operator to make use of the loco's steam by connecting the brake pipe to the table and thus lend power to this otherwise arduous task. Photomatic

Class J35 0-6-0
64482   64485   64530

Class J37 0-6-0
64575   64598   64619   64627   64634
64587   64615   64620   64631

Class J39 0-6-0
64786   64792   64892
64790   64822   64950

Class J36 0-6-0
65309   65319   65330   65333

Class J24 0-6-0
65614   65622

Class C15 4-4-2T
67461   67471

Class C16 4-4-2T
67483   67486   67490   67493   67499
67484   67489   67491   67498   67502

Class Y9 0-4-0ST
68100   68107   68110   68114   68123

Class J83 0-6-0T
68446   68452   68455   68466   68470

Class WD 2-8-0
90017   90077   90444   90515   90727
90071   90198   90463   90600
                                    Total 101

*Dundee Tay Bridge coaler in 1966 with Classes 2MT
2-6-0 No 46464 and J37 0-6-0 No 64602 (both
62B) preparing for duty. R. E. B. Siviter*

Class 3 2-6-2T
40054

Class 4 2-6-4T
42691   42692

Class 5 4-6-0
44954   45164   45384   45486

Class 2 2-6-0
46463   46464

Class A2 4-6-2
60527 *Sun Chariot*
60528 *Tudor Minstrel*

Class V2 2-6-2
60804   60822   60834   60838   60844

Class B1 4-6-0
61102   61172   61263   61292   61402
61132   61180   61278   61293

Class D34 4-4-0
62485 *Glen Murran*

Class J35 0-6-0
64530

Class J37 0-6-0
64542   64556   64587   64619   64631
64544   64575   64598   64620
64545   64585   64615   64627

Class J39 0-6-0
64786   64790   64792   64822   64950

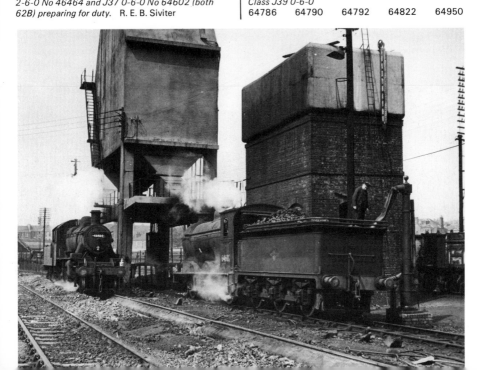

Class J36 0-6-0
65309	65319	65330	65333

Class C16 4-4-2T
67484	67490	67496	67502
67486	67491	67501	

Class J69 0-6-0T
68535

Class N15 0-6-2T
69136	69164	69204

Class 4 2-6-4T
80123	80124

Class WD 2-8-0
90444	90515

Total 64

Allocations: 1965

Class 2MT 2-6-0
46464

Class A2 4-6-2
60528 *Tudor Minstrel*
60530 *Sayajirao*
60532 *Blue Peter*

Class V2 2-6-2
60818	60836	60844	60919	60973

Class B1 4-6-0
61102	61180	61278	61340
61147	61262	61292	61403
61172	61263	61293	

Class J37 0-6-0
64547	64576	64597	64608	64624
64558	64577	64602	64620	

Class J36 0-6-0
65319

Class 4MT 2-6-4T
80124

Total 31

Tay Bridge shed lost the remainder of its steam allocation at the beginning of May 1967 when steam working on the Scottish Region was curtailed. The depot thus became one of the last seven steam venues in the Region, with all its displaced locos going to scrap. The other sheds which closed at this time were: 62C, 63A, 66A, 66B, 67A, 68D.

The ex-Caledonian shed Dundee West (see 29C London Midland Volume) stood nearby. It ranked as a sub-shed to Tay Bridge between 1951 and 1958 and housed much of the latter's allocation owing to the cramped conditions on the ex-NBR site.

62C DUNFERMLINE

Pre-Grouping Origin: North British Railway
Gazetteer Ref: 30 A3
Closed: 1967
Shed-Code: 62C (1949 to 1967)
Allocations: 1950

The western end of Dunfermline in the late 1950s showing the shed to have been re-roofed by this time. W. T. Stubbs

Class D30 4-4-0
62441 *Black Duncan*

Class D33 4-4-0
62459	62464

Class J35 0-6-0
64475	64480	64487	64496	64513
64476	64483	64493	64505	64525

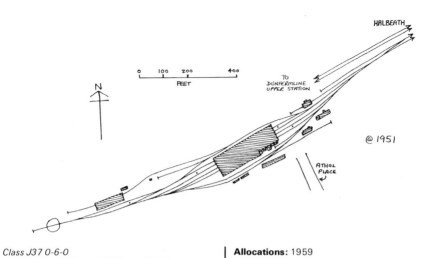

HALBEATH

0 100 200 400
FEET

To
DUNFERMLINE
UPPER STATION

@ 1951

ATHOL
PLACE

Class J37 0-6-0
64545   64560   64568   64604
64554   64561   64574   64617
64556   64567   64590   64630

Class J36 0-6-0
65239   65252
65253 *Joffre*
65281   65307   65320   65322   65323

Class J38 0-6-0
65900   65922   65926   65933
65905   65923   65928   65934
65916   65924   65930

Class C15 4-4-2T
67453   67466   67469

Class V3 2-6-2T
67669   67672

Class Y9 0-4-0ST
68101

Class J88 0-6-0T
68345   68346   68351

Class J83 0-6-0T
68465

Class J69 0-6-0T
68635

Class N15 0-6-2T
69135   69154   69164   69202   69221
69136   69160   69192   69204

Class WD 2-8-0
90117   90293   90542   90569
90199   90306   90553   90575
90278   90513   90560   90705

Total 76

Allocations: 1959

Class B1 4-6-0
61072   61101   61407

Class K2 2-6-0
61721   61758   61770

Class D30 4-4-0
62427 *Dumbiedykes*
62436 *Lord Glenvarloch*

Class J35 0-6-0
64475   64480   64493   64505   64516
64476   64487   64496   64513   64525

Class J37 0-6-0
64543   64567   64597   64617
64560   64568   64604   64630

Class J36 0-6-0
65239
65253 *Joffre*
65281   65307   65320   65323

Class J38 0-6-0
65923   65926   65930
65924   65928   65933

Class V3 2-6-2T
67669   67672

Class Y9 0-4-0ST
68101

Class J88 0-6-0T
68346   68350

Class N15 0-6-2T
69202   69221

Class WD 2-8-0
90017   90542   90553   90575   90727
90177   90547   90560   90600

Total 54

This view of 1950 shows Dunfermline's roof prior to
the BR rebuild.   J. L. Stevenson

Allocations: 1965

Class B1 4-6-0
61072   61101   61407

Class J37 0-6-0
64571   64599   64611   64623

Class J36 0-6-0
65288   65327

Class J38 0-6-0
65903   65917   65921   65931
65906   65918   65929   65934
65912   65920   65930

Class 4MT 2-6-0
76109   76110

Class WD 2-8-0
90039   90229   90515   90547
90071   90386   90534

Total 29

Dunfermline's closure coincided with the end of
steam on the Scottish Region on 1 May 1967. All its
remaining locos went for scrap as did those from the
other six depots which survived to this date (see 62B
notes). New coaling and ash plants and turntable
were brought into use in 1952 whilst the shed roof
was replaced in the mid-1950s.

63A Perth

Pre-Grouping Origin: Caledonian Railway
Gazetteer Ref: 33 F5
Closed: 1967
Shed-Codes: 29A (1948 to 1949)
63A (1949 to 1967)
Allocations: 1950

Class 4P 4-4-0
40921   40923   40939
40922   40938   41125

Class 5MT 2-6-0
42742   42743

Class 4F 0-6-0
44193   44251   44254   44258   44318
44194   44253   44257   44314   44328

Class 5MT 4-6-0

44698	44961	45086	45175	45464
44699	44972	45118	45213	45465
44704	44973	45119	45266	45466
44705	44974	45125	45309	45467
44796	44975	45127	45357	45469
44797	44976	45162	45365	45470
44801	44977	45164	45366	45472
44879	44978	45165	45389	45473
44885	44979	45166	45452	45474
44924	44980	45167	45456	45475
44925	44997	45169	45457	45483
44931	44998	45170	45458	45488
44958	44999	45171	45459	45492
44959	45007	45172	45460	45496
44960	45011	45173	45463	45497

'Jubilee' 4-6-0
45564 New South Wales
45575 Madras
45644 Howe

Class 3P 4-4-0

54447	54459	54476	54494	54501
54448	54467	54485	54499	54502
54458	54469	54489	54500	54503

Class 2P 0-4-4T

| 55144 | 55175 | 55208 | 55212 | 55216 |
| 55171 | 55176 | 55209 | 55213 | 55218 |

Class 3F 0-6-0T

| 56246 | 56328 | 56347 | 56353 |
| 56290 | 56331 | 56352 | 56359 |

A general view of Perth in 1966 looking south from the nearby A90 Edinburgh Road.   K. Fairey

Class 2F 0-6-0

| 57339 | 57345 | 57450 | 57473 |

Class D49 4-4-0
62714 Perthshire
62725 Inverness-shire

Class WD 2-8-0

| 90523 | 90530 | 90675 |

Total 138

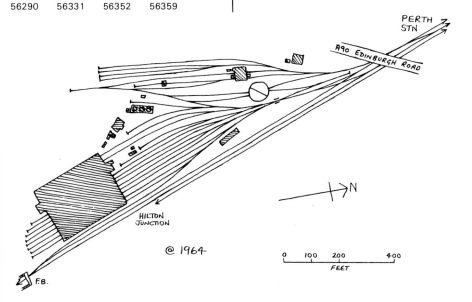

PERTH STN

A90 EDINBURGH ROAD

→N

HILTON JUNCTION

@ 1964

F.B.

| 0 | 100 | 200 | | 400 |
FEET

Allocations: 1959

Class 4 2-6-4T
42168	42169	42271

Class 6P5F 2-6-0
42800	42801

Class 4F 0-6-0
44253	44257	44314
44254	44258	44328

Class 5 4-6-0
44698	44885	44997	45366	45474
44699	44921	44998	45367	45475
44704	44924	44999	45452	45483
44705	44925	45047	45458	45488
44720	44931	45053	45459	45492
44721	44959	45165	45463	45496
44796	44960	45168	45465	45497
44797	44961	45170	45467	
44801	44978	45171	45470	
44820	44979	45172	45472	
44879	44980	45365	45473	

An elevated view of the depot as seen from the coaling plant in 1954. Photomatic

A quartet of Class A4 Pacifics at Perth in 1965 by which time the survivors had been reduced to eight. Left to right are Nos 60009 Union of South Africa, *60026* Miles Beevor, *60019* Bittern *(all 61B) and 60031* Golden Plover *(65B).* K. R. Pirt

'Jubilee' 4-6-0
45673	*Keppel*
45692	*Cyclops*
45727	*Inflexible*

Class 3P 4-4-0
54467	54485	54489	54499	54503
54469	54486	54494	54500	

Class 2P 0-4-4T
55200	55209	55218	55230

Class 3F 0-6-0T
56246	56290	56331	56347	56359

Class 2F 0-6-0
57345	57424	57473

Class D34 4-4-0
62470	*Glen Roy*
62484	*Glen Lyon*

Class 5 4-6-0

73005	73007	73009	73107
73006	73008	73106	73120

Class 4 2-6-4T
80126

Total 97

Allocations: 1965

Class 5MT 4-6-0

44698	44724	44925	44979	45461
44704	44797	44931	44980	45472
44705	44799	44959	44997	45473
44720	44879	44960	44998	45474
44722	44924	44978	45047	45475

Class 4MT 2-6-4T

80028	80092	80093	80126

Total 29

Perth in the late 1950s with its usual predominance of 'Black Fives'. W. T. Stubbs

A notable feature of Perth's allocation throughout the BR period was the high proportion of 'Black Five' 4-6-0s shedded there.

Like the previous two depots, Perth survived until the end of steam on the Scottish Region and lost all its remaining locos to scrap in May 1967 (see 62B notes).

63B STIRLING SOUTH

Pre-Grouping Origin: Caledonian Railway
Gazetteer Ref: 30 A5
Closed: 1966
Shed-Codes: 31B (1948 to 1949)
63B (1949 to 1960)
65J (1960 to 1966)
Allocations: 1950 (63B)

The southern end of Stirling South in 1954 with ex-Caley tank and tender classes well represented. Note that the turntable had been filled in by this time. Photomatic

Stirling South from the north in 1953. B. Hilton

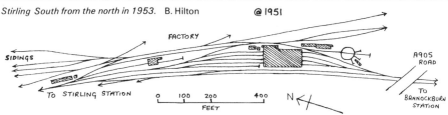

@ 1951

FACTORY

SIDINGS

TO STIRLING STATION

0   100   200   400

FEET

N

A905
ROAD

TO
BANNOCKBURN
STATION

Class 4P 4-4-0				
40913	40924			

Class 4MT 2-6-4T				
42198	42199			

Class 4F 0-6-0				
44011	44283	44322	44330	44331

Class 5MT 4-6-0		
45016	45358	45359

Class 2P 0-4-4T			
55122	55126	55145	55222

*LMS Class 2P 0-4-4T No 15122 (eventual BR
No 55122) (63B) outside the south entrance to
Stirling South shed in 1950.* W. Potter

Class 3F 0-6-0T				
56232	56254	56343	56365	56366

Class 2F 0-6-0				
57232	57246	57264	57424	57468
57233	57252	57283	57425	
57243	57257	57423	57460	

Class D1 4-4-0
62209

Class D30 4-4-0
62426 *Cuddie Headrigg*

Class D33 4-4-0
62461

Class J35 0-6-0				
64461	64471	64497	64501	64520

Class J37 0-6-0
64542   64544   64569   64585

Class C15 4-4-2T
67462

Classes V1 & V3* 2-6-2T
67650   67675*

Total 49

Allocations: 1959 (63B)

Class 4 2-6-4T
42198   42199   42690   42693

Class 5 4-6-0
45016   45213   45359   45400
45049   45214   45389   45423
45084   45357   45396   45487

Class 3P 4-4-0
54476   54504

Class 2P 0-4-4T
55195   55222

Class 3F 0-6-0T
56232   56343   56365

Class 2F 0-6-0
57232   57243   57252   57264   57324
57233   57246   57257   57276   57339

Class 3F 0-6-0
57576   57642   57679

Class D30 4-4-0
62426 Cuddie Headrigg

Class D49 4-4-0
62714 Perthshire

Class 4 2-6-4T
80125

Total 39

Allocations: 1965 (65J)

Class 5MT 4-6-0
45016   45213   45357   45389   45423
45084   45214   45359   45396

Total 9

Stirling South closed to steam in June 1966 and its last remaining engine, Class 5MT 4-6-0 No 73154, transferred to Motherwell (66B). The depot was used for loco storage after this date. The other shed at Stirling was Shore Road (ex-NBR) which served as a sub-shed to South until 1958.

63C FORFAR

Pre-Grouping Origin: Caledonian Railway
Gazetteer Ref: 34 D4
Closed: 1964
Shed-Codes: 29D (1948 to 1949)
63C (1949 to 1958)
Allocations: 1950

Forfar in 1955 as viewed from the nearby roadbridge. D. B. Swale

The western end of Forfar in 1959 by which time it had become a sub-shed to 63A Perth. On display here are Classes 2P 0-4-4T No 55209 and 3P 4-4-0 No 54489 (both 63A). Photomatic

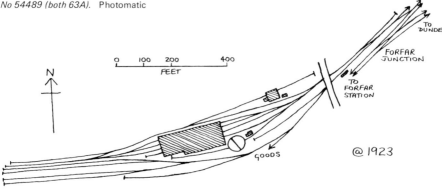

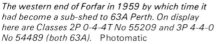

@ 1923

Class 5MT 2-6-0
42738   42800   42801

Class 3P 4-4-0
54450   54454   54486

Class 2P 0-4-4T

55136	55169	55193	55200
55161	55172	55194	55214
55162	55185	55195	55230

Class 2F 0-6-0
57324   57368   57441

Total 21

The west entrance of Forfar depot in 1953 depicting Class 4P 4-4-0 No 40939 (63C) outside. B. Hilton

Forfar lost its code in November 1958 and became sub-shed to Perth (63A) until July 1964, when upon closure, the locos moved to the latter, parent depot.

63D FORT WILLIAM

Looking north-west to Fort William shed and yard in 1960 with (left to right) 'K1', 'Black Five' and 'B1' examples nearest the camera.   K. Fairey

Pre-Grouping Origin: North British Railway
Gazetteer Ref: 32 C3
Closed: 1962
Shed-Codes: 63D (1949 to 1955)
65J (1955 to 1960)
63B (1960 to 1962)
Allocations: 1950 (63D)

Class K2 2-6-0
61782 *Loch Eil*
61783 *Loch Sheil*
61787 *Loch Quoich*
61788 *Loch Rannoch*
61789 *Loch Laidon*
61790 *Loch Lomond*
61791 *Loch Laggan*

Black Five 4-6-0 No 44975 (63B) stands alone in Fort William shed in 1960.   K. Fairey

This 1957 view from the rear of Fort William portrays Class K2 2-6-0 No 61794 Loch Oich (65A) at rest beside the turntable.   Real Photos

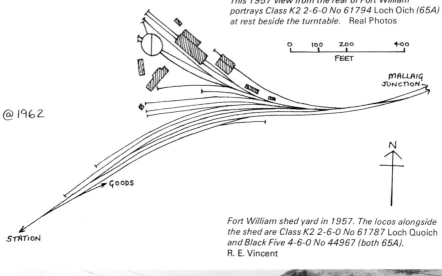

@1962

MALLAIG JUNCTION

GOODS

STATION

0   100   200   400
FEET

N

Fort William shed yard in 1957. The locos alongside the shed are Class K2 2-6-0 No 61787 Loch Quoich and Black Five 4-6-0 No 44967 (both 65A).
R. E. Vincent

Class K4 2-6-0
61995 *Cameron of Locheil*
61996 *Lord of the Isles*

Class J36 0-6-0
65237   65300   65313

Total 12

Allocations: 1959 (65J)

Class 4F 0-6-0
44255

Class 5 4-6-0
44972   44974   44976
44973   44975   44977

Class K2 2-6-0
61784
61791 *Loch Laggan*

Class K1 2-6-0
61997 *MacCailin Mor*
62011   62031   62052
62012   62034
Class J36 0-6-0
65300   65313

Total 17

Closing in December 1962 as 63B, Fort William's few steam engines transferred to North Eastern Region stock.

63E OBAN

Pre-Grouping Origin: Caledonian Railway
Gazetteer Ref: 32 F4
Closed: 1962
Shed-Codes: 31C (1948 to 1949)
63E (1949 to 1955)
63D (1955 to 1959)
63C (1959 to 1962)
Allocations: 1950 (63E)

Class 2P 0-4-4T
55187   55196   55198   55215   55263

Class 2F 0-6-0
57254   57396

Total 7

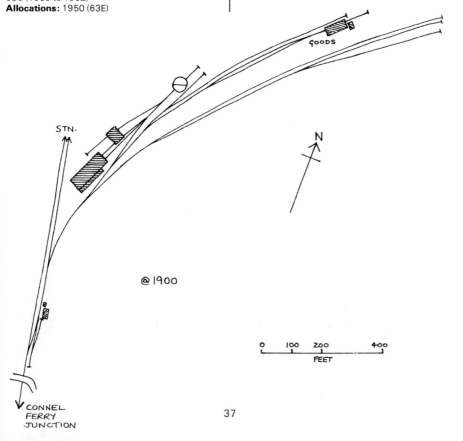

STN.

GOODS

N

@ 1900

0   100   200   400
FEET

CONNEL
FERRY
JUNCTION

A bird's eye view of Oban shed and goods yard in 1927. H. C. Casserley

Allocations: 1959 (63D)

Class 2P 0-4-4T
55126   55208   55215   55220   55263

Class 3F 0-6-0
57571   57667

Total 7

A south-westerley view of Oban in 1952 with two 'Black Fives' peering within. H. C. Casserley

At closure in July 1962, Oban's last few engines went to Perth 63A.

64A ST MARGARETS

Pre-Grouping Origin: North British Railway
Gazetteer Ref: 30 B2
Closed: 1967
Shed-Code: 64A (1949 to 1967)
Allocations: 1950

Class 5MT 4-6-0
45036   45085

Class 2MT 2-6-0
46460   46461   46462

Class 2F 0-6-0T
47162

Class V2 2-6-2
60825   60848   60953
60836   60894   60980

*St Margarets main building in 1960 with Classes V3
2-6-2T No 67670, V1 2-6-2T No 67649 and V2
2-6-2 No 60825 (all 64A) facing the camera.*
K. Fairey

Class B1 4-6-0
61002 *Impala*
61061   61067
61242 *Alexander Reith Gray*
61277   61354   61356   61358
61341   61355   61357   61359

Class K3 2-6-0
61823   61879   61909   61931   61988
61855   61881   61911   61933   61990
61857   61885   61916   61955   61991
61876   61897   61924   61968   61992
61878   61900   61928   61983

Class D30 4-4-0
62421 *Laird O' Monkbarns*
62424 *Claverhouse*
62435 *Norna*

Class D32 4-4-0
62451

Class D34 4-4-0
62471 *Glen Falloch*
62483 *Glen Garry*
62484 *Glen Lyon*
62487 *Glen Arklet*
62488 *Glen Aladale*
62490 *Glen Fintaig*
62494 *Glen Gour*

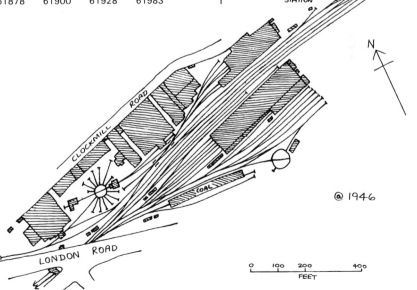

PIERSHILL
JUNCTION

PIERSHILL
STATION

N

CLOCKMILL ROAD

COAL

@ 1946

LONDON ROAD

0   100   200   400
FEET

TO
ABBEYHILL
JUNCTION

Class A4 4-6-2 No 60027 Merlin *(64A) alongside the coal stage at St Margarets in June 1965 looking rather forlorn. The diagonal stripe on the cabside was in indication that the loco was not to work on electrified lines.* Merlin *was withdrawn in September of the same year and the class as a whole were defunct by September 1966.* K. Fairey

Class D49 4-4-0
62702 *Oxfordshire*
62711 *Dumbartonshire*
62712 *Morayshire*
62715 *Roxburghshire*
62721 *Warwickshire*

Class J35 0-6-0

64462	64492	64517	64524	64535
64479	64506	64518	64527	
64486	64512	64519	64532	
64489	64515	64523	64533	

Class J37 0-6-0

64538	64562	64586	64606	64636
64543	64566	64594	64607	64637
64547	64552	64595	64608	
64552	64576	64599	64614	
64555	64577	64603	64624	
64557	64582	64605	64625	

Class J39 0-6-0

64794	64946	64963	64986

Class J36 0-6-0
65224 *Mons*

65251	65286	65305	65316
65258	65288	65310	65334
65267	65292	65311	

Class J24 0-6-0

65617 65623

Class J38 0-6-0

65906	65914	65918	65920	65929
65912	65915	65919	65927	

Class C16 4-4-2T

67492	67494	67495	67496	67497

Class V1 2-6-2T

67605	67608	67624	67649	67668
67606	67609	67629	67659	67670
67607	67617	67630	67666	

Looking north-east across the turntable of the old 'tank' roundhouse at St Margarets in 1958. Left to right are Classes J88 0-6-0T No 68342 and J83 0-6-0T Nos 68472 and 68449 (all 64A). K. Fairey

St Margarets shed in 1947 from a westerly viewpoint. W. Potter

Class Y9 0-4-0ST

68092	68096	68099	68111	68122
68093	68097	68102	68115	
68095	68098	68105	68119	

Class J88 0-6-0T

68320	68334	68340	68348
68325	68338	68342	68352

Class J83 0-6-0T

68448	68450	68463	68469	68474
68449	68454	68464	68472	68477

Class J67* & J69 0-6-0T

68492*	68511*	68562
68505	68525	68623

Class J50 0-6-0T

68952

Class N15 0-6-2T

69130	69141	69148	69168	69186
69133	69144	69149	69172	69219
69134	69146	69152	69173	
69140	69147	69167	69175	

Class WD 2-8-0

90038	90289	90436	90493
90114	90291	90468	90496
90248	90376	90469	90555

Total 221

Allocations: 1959

Class 2 2-6-0

46461   46462

Class 2F 0-6-0T

47162

Class V2 2-6-2

60813	60823	60836
60818	60825	60840

60873 Coldstreamer

60882	60894	60933	60958	60971
60883	60900	60937	60965	60980
60892	60931	60953	60969	

Class B1 4-6-0

61029 Chamois

61099	61108	61184	61191

61246 Lord Balfour of Burleigh

61260	61332	61351	61357	61398
61307	61341	61354	61359	
61308	61349	61356	61397	

Class K3 2-6-0

61823	61881	61924	61968	61992
61855	61885	61928	61983	
61876	61900	61931	61988	
61878	61909	61933	61990	
61879	61911	61955	61991	

Class D30 4-4-0

62421 Laird O' Monkbarns

Class D34 4-4-0

62471 Glen Falloch
62487 Glen Arklet
62488 Glen Aladale

Class D49 4-4-0

62711 Dumbartonshire
62715 Roxburghshire
62718 Kinross-shire

Class J35 0-6-0

64462	64483	64515	64523	64533
64479	64489	64518	64524	64535
64482	64506	64519	64532	

Class J37 0-6-0

64536	64562	64586	64601	64612
64538	64566	64590	64603	64613
64547	64572	64591	64605	64614
64552	64576	64594	64606	64624
64555	64577	64595	64607	64625
64557	64582	64599	64608	64637

Class J39 0-6-0

64795   64975

Class J36 0-6-0

65224 Mons

65258	65288	65327	65329	65334

41

Class J38 0-6-0
65906	65915	65919	65927
65912	65916	65920	65929
65914	65918	65922	65934

Class C16 4-4-2T
67492	67497

Class V1 * & V3 2-6-2T
67617	67649*	67666*	67670
67624	67659*	67668	

Class Y9 0-4-0ST
68095	68119

Class J88 0-6-0T
68320	68325	68338	68342

Class J83 0-6-0T
68448	68454	68470	68472	68477

Class J72 0-6-0T
69013	69014

Class N15 0-6-2T
69133	69144	69152	69185
69134	69146	69154	69186
69135	69149	69168	69219
69141	69150	69173	69222

Class 2 2-6-0
78048	78049

Total 175

Allocations: 1965

Class 4MT 2-6-4T
42128	42691

Class 2MT 2-6-0
46462

Class A4 4-6-2
60024 *Kingfisher*
60027 *Merlin*

Class A3 4-6-2
60041 *Salmon Trout*
60052 *Prince Palatine*
60100 *Spearmint*

Class V2 2-6-2
60813	60824	60846	60955
60816	60835	60931	60970

Class B1 4-6-0
61029 *Chamois*
61076	61099	61191

61244 *Strang Steel*
61324	61345	61350	61357	61397
61344	61349	61354	61396	61404

Class J36 0-6-0
65234

Class 4MT 2-6-4T
80006	80022	80054	80114
80007	80026	80055	80122

Total 40

Most of the sheds steam stock was withdrawn late in 1966, but closure came in April 1967 when the last engine, No 65234 went for scrap.

64B HAYMARKET

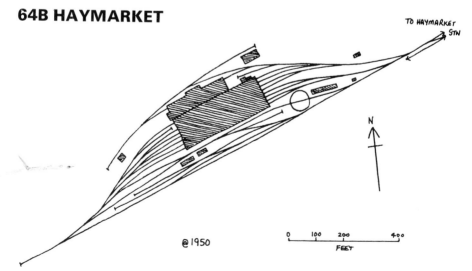

@ 1950

TO HAYMARKET STN

N

0	100	200	400

FEET

Pre-Grouping Origin: North British Railway
Gazetteer Ref: 30 inset
Closed: 1963
Shed-Code: 64B (1949 to 1963)
Allocations: 1950

The western end of Haymarket in 1952 with the following classes on parade (left to right) 4MT 2-6-0, J35 0-6-0, D11 4-4-0, D49 4-4-0, A1 4-6-2 and V2 2-6-2. J. L. Stevenson

Class A4 4-6-2
60004 *William Whitelaw*
60009 *Union of South Africa*
60011 *Dominion of India*
60012 *Commonwealth of Australia*
60024 *Kingfisher*
60027 *Merlin*
60031 *Golden Plover*

Class A3 4-6-2
60035 *Windsor Lad*
60037 *Hyperion*
60041 *Salmon Trout*
60043 *Brown Jack*
60057 *Ormonde*
60087 *Blenheim*
60090 *Grand Parade*
60094 *Colorado*
60096 *Papyrus*
60097 *Humorist*
60098 *Spion Kop*
60099 *Call Boy*
60100 *Spearmint*
60101 *Cicero*

Class A1 4-6-2
60152 *Holyrood*
60159 *Bonnie Dundee*
60160 *Auld Reekie*
60161 *North British*
60162 *Saint Johnstoun*

Class A2 4-6-2
60507 *Highland Chieftain*
60509 *Waverley*
60510 *Robert the Bruce*
60519 *Honeyway*
60529 *Pearl Diver*
60530 *Sayajirao*
60532 *Blue Peter*
60534 *Irish Elegance*
60535 *Hornet's Beauty*
60536 *Trimbush*

Class V2 2-6-2

60816	60882	60951	60972
60834	60927	60959	

Class B1 4-6-0
61007 *Klipspringer*

61076	61081	61178

61221 *Sir Alexander Erskine-Hill*
61244 *Strang Steel*
61245 *Murray of Elibank*

Class D29 & D30 4-4-0*
62405* *The Fair Maid*
62437 *Adam Woodcock*

Class D11 4-4-0
62677 *Edie Ochiltree*
62678 *Luckie Mucklebackit*
62679 *Lord Glenallan*
62683 *Hobbie Elliott*
62685 *Malcolm Graeme*
62690 *The Lady of the Lake*
62691 *Laird of Balmawhapple*
62692 *Allan-Bane*
62693 *Roderick Dhu*
62694 *James Fitzjames*

Class D49 4-4-0
62705 *Lanarkshire*
62706 *Forfarshire*
62709 *Berwickshire*
62719 *Peebles-shire*
62733 *Northumberland*

Class J36 0-6-0
65240
65243 *Maude*

Class V1 2-6-2T

67610	67615	67620

Class J88 0-6-0T

68328	68339

Class J83 0-6-0T

68457	68460	68473	68478	68481

Class N15 0-6-2T

69169	69220

Total 81

43

Allocations: 1959

Class 2P 0-4-4T
55165

Class A4 4-6-2
60004 *William Whitelaw*
60009 *Union of South Africa*
60011 *Empire of India*
60012 *Commonwealth of Australia*
60024 *Kingfisher*
60027 *Merlin*
60031 *Golden Plover*

Class A3 4-6-2
60035 *Windsor Lad*
60037 *Hyperion*
60041 *Salmon Trout*
60043 *Brown Jack*
60057 *Ormonde*
60087 *Blenheim*
60089 *Felsted*
60090 *Grand Parade*
60094 *Colorado*
60096 *Papyrus*
60097 *Humorist*
60098 *Spion Kop*
60099 *Call Boy*
60100 *Spearmint*
60101 *Cicero*

Class A1 4-6-2
60152 *Holyrood*
60159 *Bonnie Dundee*
60160 *Auld Reekie*
60161 *North British*
60162 *Saint Johnstoun*

Class A2 4-6-2
60507 *Highland Chieftain*
60509 *Waverley*
60510 *Robert the Bruce*
60519 *Honeyway*
60529 *Pearl Diver*
60530 *Sayajirao*
60534 *Irish Elegance*
60535 *Hornet's Beauty*
60536 *Trimbush*
60537 *Bachelor's Button*

A 1954 view of Haymarket's Eastern end.
Photomatic

Class V2 2-6-2

| 60816 | 60824 | 60920 | 60951 | 60959 |
| 60819 | 60827 | 60927 | 60957 | |

Class B1 4-6-0
61007 *Kilpspringer*

| 61076 | 61081 | 61178 | 61219 |

61221 *Sir Alexander Erskine-Hill*
61244 *Strang Steel*
61245 *Murray of Elibank*

Class D11 4-4-0
62685 *Malcolm Graeme*
62690 *The Lady of the Lake*
62691 *Laird of Balmawhapple*
62692 *Allan-Bane*
62693 *Roderick Dhu*
62694 *James Fitzjames*

Class D49 4-4-0
62705 *Lanarkshire*
62709 *Berwickshire*
62719 *Peebles-shire*
62743 *The Cleveland*

Class J36 0-6-0
65235 *Gough*
65243 *Maude*

Class V1* & V3 2-6-2T
67610*   67615   67620

Class J83 0-6-0T
68457   68481

Class N15 0-6-2T
69211

Total 73

With almost three-quarters of its allocation consisting of named engines, Haymarket was the 'mecca' for spotters in the Scottish capital. Its main role was to provide and service top-link locomotives for Waverley expresses.

Steam closure came in September 1963 when the remaining engines transferred to Dalry Road (64C) and St Margarets (64A).

44

64C DALRY ROAD

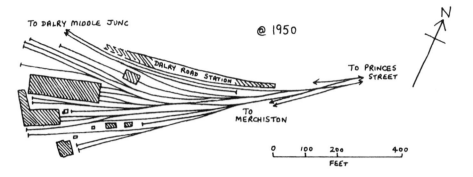

@ 1950

To DALRY MIDDLE JUNC

DALRY ROAD STATION

To PRINCES STREET

To MERCHISTON

| 0 | 100 | 200 | | 400 |

FEET

N

Pre-Grouping Origin: Caledonian Railway
Gazetteer Ref: 30 inset
Closed: 1965
Shed-Codes: 28B (1948 to 1949)
64C (1949 to 1965)
Allocations: 1950

Class 4P 4-4-0
40911   41177   41178

Class 4MT 2-6-4T
42268   42270   42272
42269   42271   42273

Class 5MT 2-6-0
42804   42807   42830

Class 5MT 4-6-0
45022   45023   45029   45184   45362

Class 2F 0-6-0T
47163

Class 3P 4-4-0
54451   54452   54478

Class 2P 0-4-4T
55139   55166   55189   55210
55165   55177   55202   55229

Class 3F 0-6-0T
56253   56283   56312   56313

Class 3F 0-6-0
57550   57559   57576   57654
57553   57565   57645

*Edinburgh Dalry Road as viewed from the east in
1954. The shed had an unexpected delivery in this
year, namely brand new Class 3MT 2-6-0 No 77011.
It didn't stay long however as it was discovered that
the loco should have been sent to Darlington!*
Photomatic

45

Two of Dalry's Class 2P 0-4-4 tanks alongside the coaler on the station side in 1947. They eventually became BR Nos 55229 and 55210 and continued to serve the depot until their withdrawal in 1961.
W. Potter

Allocations: 1959

Class 4 2-6-4T
42270   42272   42273

Class 6P5F 2-6-0
42807

Class J37 0-6-0
64536   64591

Class 5 4-6-0
44994   45023   45036   45127   45183
45022   45030   45086   45155

Class J36 0-6-0
65271

Class N15 0-6-2T
69187

Total 44

Edinburgh Dalry Road yard from the South in 1962. Locos on view are Nos 42273, 76105, 57654, 45036 and 55124.   D. J. Dippie

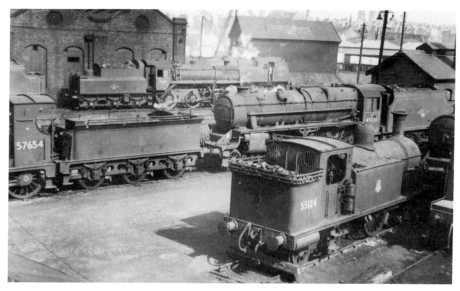

Class 2F 0-6-0T
47163

Class 3P 4-4-0
54478

Class 2P 0-4-4T
55202   55210   55229   55233

Class 3F 0-6-0T
56312   56313

Class 3F 0-6-0
57550   57560   57645
57559   57565   57654

Class J35 0-6-0
64497   64500   64501   64527

Class J37 0-6-0
64554   64561   64569

Class J39 0-6-0
64794   64946   64963   64986

Class N15 0-6-2T
69187

Total 39

Allocations: 1965

Class 4MT 2-6-4T
42273

Class 5MT 4-6-0
44702   45053   45162   45360   45477
44975   45127   45168   45469   45483

Class B1 4-6-0
61134
61245 Murray of Elibank
61307   61308   61347

Total 16

At closure in October 1965 the few remaining locos transferred to St Margarets (64A).

64D CARSTAIRS

Pre-Grouping Origin: Caledonian Railway
Gazetteer Ref: 30 D4
Closed: 1966
Shed-Codes: 28C (1948 to 1949)
64D (1949 to 1960)
66E (1960 to 1966)
Allocations: 1950 (64D)

Class 2P 4-4-0
40592

Class 4P 4-4-0
40901   40907   41136   41147
40903   41130   41145   41180

Class 4MT 2-6-4T
42162   42163   42173   42174   42217

A 1957 view of Carstairs eastern end with Class 3P 4-4-0 No 54505 (64D) in the right foregound.
J. L. Stevenson

Looking east to the opposite end of Carstairs in 1950 with (left to right) 5MT 4-6-0 No 45117 (64D), an unidentified 3F 0-6-0, 4MT 2-6-4T No 42162 (64D) and 3F 0-6-0 No 57655 (64D). J. L. Stevenson

TO CARNWATH
AND BANKHEAD
STATIONS

DOLPHINTON
JUNCTION

STRAWFRANK
JUNCTION

STN

0   100   200   400
FEET

@ 1941

N

STATION

TO LANARK

48

Class 5MT 4-6-0
44700	44952	44955	45117
44701	44953	45087	45161

Class 3P 4-4-0
54438	54449	54477	54505
54446	54461	54490	

Class 2P 0-4-4T
55261

Class 2F 0-6-0
57323	57385	57438
57340	57386	57451

Class 3F 0-6-0
57583	57608	57626	57670
57603	57613	57635	57679
57604	57618	57655	

Class J36 0-6-0
65329

Class WD 2-10-0
90753	90768

Total 50

Allocations: 1959 (64D)

Class 4 2-6-4T
42142	42162	42173	42204	42217
42145	42163	42177	42216	

Class 5 4-6-0
44700	44952	45011	45173	45245
44701	44953	45087	45174	
44793	44955	45166	45175	

Class 3P 4-4-0
54461	54477	54490	54505

Class 2P 0-4-4T
55261

Class 2F 0-6-0
57385	57386	57451

Class 3F 0-6-0
57583	57608	57618	57635	57670
57604	57613	57626	57655	

Class WD 2-10-0
90753	90768

Total 41

Allocations: 1965 (66E)

Class 4MT 2-6-4T
42058	42125	42169	42274

Class 5MT 4-6-0
44700	44954	45011	45309
44952	44956	45090	45478
44953	44973	45245	45492

Total 16

Carstairs lost its allocation in December 1966, all engines being withdrawn.

64E POLMONT

Pre-Grouping Origin: North British Railway
Gazetteer Ref: 30 B4
Closed: 1964
Shed-Codes: 64E (1949 to 1960)
65K (1960 to 1964)
Allocations: 1950 (64E)

Class J35 0-6-0
64484	64490	64502	64528

Class J37 0-6-0
64537	64553	64571	64589	64593
64551	64570	64588	64592	64613

Polmont from the west in 1956 showing three of its Class J36 0-6-0's and a solitary J35 0-6-0.
J. L. Stevenson

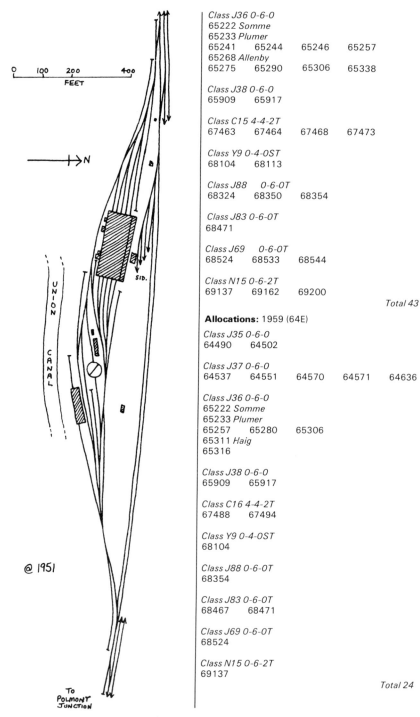

```
0    100   200        400
|----|----|----------|
        FEET
```

⊢→N

@ 1951

UNION CANAL

SID.

To
POLMONT
JUNCTION

Class J36 0-6-0
65222 *Somme*
65233 *Plumer*
65241   65244   65246   65257
65268 *Allenby*
65275   65290   65306   65338

Class J38 0-6-0
65909   65917

Class C15 4-4-2T
67463   67464   67468   67473

Class Y9 0-4-0ST
68104   68113

Class J88   0-6-0T
68324   68350   68354

Class J83 0-6-0T
68471

Class J69   0-6-0T
68524   68533   68544

Class N15 0-6-2T
69137   69162   69200

Total 43

Allocations: 1959 (64E)

Class J35 0-6-0
64490   64502

Class J37 0-6-0
64537   64551   64570   64571   64636

Class J36 0-6-0
65222 *Somme*
65233 *Plumer*
65257   65280   65306
65311 *Haig*
65316

Class J38 0-6-0
65909   65917

Class C16 4-4-2T
67488   67494

Class Y9 0-4-0ST
68104

Class J88 0-6-0T
68354

Class J83 0-6-0T
68467   68471

Class J69 0-6-0T
68524

Class N15 0-6-2T
69137

Total 24

50

The shed closed in May 1964 and its remaining locos went to Grangemouth (65F).

The eastern end of Polmont in 1955 with Classes J69 0-6-0T No 68524 (left) and 4MT 2-6-0 No 43141 (both 64E). The shed possessed two of this latter class in this year, the other being No 43140.   J. L. Stevenson

64F BATHGATE

Pre-Grouping Origin: North British Railway
Gazetteer Ref: 30 C4
Closed: 1966
Shed-Code: 64F (1949 to 1966)
Allocations: 1950

Class D31 4-4-0
62283

Class D30 4-4-0
62439 *Father Ambrose*

Class D34 4-4-0
62495 *Glen Luss*

Class J35 0-6-0
| 64468 | 64491 | 64504 | 64510 | 64529 |

Class J36 0-6-0
65211	65229	65231		
65225	65230	65234		
65235 *Gough*				
65248	65265	65280	65318	65344
65250	65276	65282	65327	65346
65254	65277	65303	65341	
65261	65278	65314	65342	

Class N15 0-6-2T
| 69142 | 69156 | 69158 | 69159 | 69216 |

Total 38

The original six road structure at Bathgate in 1950. It was reported that the depot was in a bad state of repair at this time due to subsidence. In 1954 a new four road structure was built on the same site. J. L. Stevenson

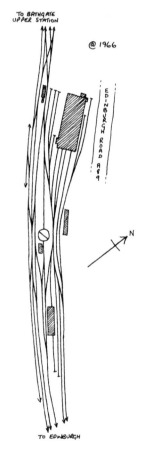

TO BATHGATE
UPPER STATION

@ 1966

EDINBURGH ROAD A89

N

TO EDINBURGH

0 100 200 400
FEET

The rebuilt four road Bathgate in 1956 with six-coupled types dominating the scene.
J. L. Stevenson

Allocations: 1959

Class 4 2-6-0
43138

Class D30 4-4-0
62439 *Father Ambrose*

Class D34 4-4-0
62495 *Glen Luss*

Class J35 0-6-0

64468	64491	64510	64529
64484	64504	64512	

Class J37 0-6-0

64553	64583	64634

Class J36 0-6-0

65229	65230	65259	65261	65265
65268 *Allenby*				
65276	65282	65318	65342	65346
65277	65290	65341	65344	

Class N15 0-6-2T

69156	69159	69216

Total 31

Allocations: 1965

Class J36 0-6-0
65243 *Maude*

65267	65282	65297

Class 4MT 2-6-0

76104	76105	76106	76107	76111

Class 2MT 2-6-0

78045	78046	78050	78052	78054

Total 14

Although Bathgate officially closed to steam in August 1966, the last engine was not transferred away until December the same year.

Bathgate shed in 1959 with an unidentified visiting Class V2 2-6-2 sandwiched between 0-6-0 types.
Photomatic

64G HAWICK

Pre-Grouping Origin: North British Railway
Gazetteer Ref: 31 F1
Closed: 1966
Shed-Code: 64G (1949 to 1966)
Allocations: 1950

Class D30 4-4-0
62417 *Hal o' the Wynd*
62420 *Dominie Sampson*
62422 *Caleb Balderstone*
62423 *Dugald Dalgetty*
62425 *Ellangowan*
62428 *The Talisman*
62432 *Quentin Durward*
62440 *Wandering Willie*

Class J35 0-6-0
64463   64494   64509

Class J37 0-6-0
64539

Class J36 0-6-0
65232   65259   65317
65242   65279   65340

Class C15 4-4-2T
67457   67459   67465   67472   67477

Class YI 0-4-0T
68138

Total 24

Looking west to Hawick MPD in 1952 with a good cross section of its allocation on display. Left to right are Classes J36 0-6-0 No 65232, C15 4-4-2T No 67477 and D30 4-4-0 No 62423 Dugald Dalgetty.   J. L. Stevenson

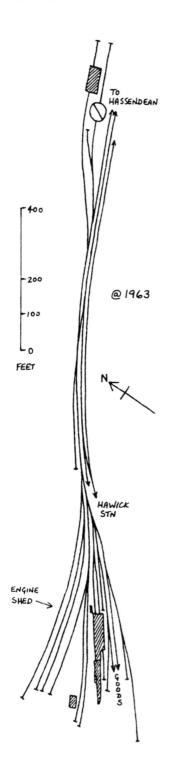

TO
HASSENDEAN

@ 1963

┌ 400

├ 200

├ 100

└ 0
FEET

N

HAWICK
STN

ENGINE
SHED →

GOODS

Allocations: 1959

Class 4 2-6-0
43141

Class D34 4-4-0
62483 *Glen Garry*
62494 *Glen Gour*

Class J35 0-6-0
64463   64494   64509

Class J37 0-6-0
64539

Class J36 0-6-0
65234   65275   65317   65331

Class C16 4-4-2T
67489

Class V3 2-6-2T
67606

Class N2 0-6-2T
69510

Class 2 2-6-0
78046   78047

Total 16

Classes D30 4-4-0 No 62432 Quentin Durward *and J36 0-6-0 No 65331 (both 64G) share a road outside Hawick depot in 1953.*   B. K. B. Green

Allocations: 1965

Class 4MT 2-6-0
76049   76050

Class 2MT 2-6-0
78047   78049

Class 4MT 2-6-4T
80113

Total 5

Hawick shed in 1958. B. Hilton

Hawick closed in January 1966 its remaining engines transferred to St Margarets (64A).

As will be seen from the diagram, a bad design feature of Hawick was the positioning of the turntable before the coaling plant. Thus, whenever the former was inoperative, locos could not gain access to the latter and had to be coaled in a more primitive manner.

65A EASTFIELD

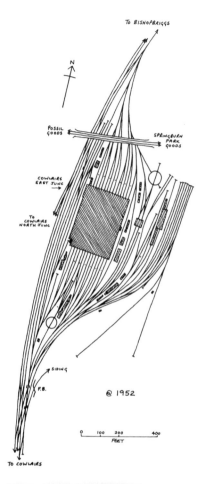

To BISHOPBRIGGS

N

POSSIL GOODS

SPRINGBURN PARK GOODS

COWLAIRS EAST JUNC

To COWLAIRS NORTH JUNC

SIDING

F.B.

@ 1952

0 100 200 400
FEET

To COWLAIRS

Pre-Grouping Origin: North British Railway
Gazetteer Ref: 44 D4
Closed: 1966
Shed-Code: 65A (1949 to 1966)
Allocations: 1950

Class 5MT 4-6-0
45010

Class B1 4-6-0
61064	61117	61180		
61116	61172	61197		
61243 *Sir Harold Mitchell*				
61260	61261	61340	61342	61344

Class V4 2-6-2
61700 *Bantam Cock*
61701

Class K2 2-6-0
61764 *Loch Arkaig*
61774 *Loch Garry*
61775 *Loch Treig*
61776	61779			
61781 *Loch Morar*				
61784	61785	61786	61792	61793
61794 *Loch Oich*				

Classes KI* & K4 2-6-0
61993 *Loch Long*
61994 *The Great Marquess*
61997* *MacCailin Mor*
61998 *MacLeod of MacLeod*

Class D33 4-4-0
62460	62462

A general view of the southern approaches to Eastfield in 1954 as seen from the footbridge which gave access. Photomatic

A 1955 view from the north with the following Eastfield locos facing (left to right) Classes B1 4-6-0 No 61117, D34 4-4-0 No 62496 Glen Loy, N15 0-6-2T No 69163 and J36 0-6-0 No 65221.
D. B. Swale

Class D34 4-4-0
62469 *Glen Douglas*
62470 *Glen Roy*
62472 *Glen Nevis*
62474 *Glen Croe*
62477 *Glen Dochart*
62479 *Glen Sheil*
62480 *Glen Fruin*
62482 *Glen Mamie*
62489 *Glen Dessary*
62493 *Glen Gloy*
62496 *Glen Loy*
62497 *Glen Mallie*
62498 *Glen Moidart*

Class D11 4-4-0
62671 *Bailie MacWheeble*
62672 *Baron of Bradwardine*
62673 *Evan Dhu*
62674 *Flora MacIvor*
62675 *Colonel Gardiner*
62676 *Jonathan Oldbuck*
62680 *Lucy Ashton*
62681 *Captain Craigengelt*
62682 *Haystoun of Bucklaw*
62684 *Wizard of the Moor*
62686 *The Fiery Cross*
62687 *Lord James of Douglas*
62688 *Ellen Douglas*
62689 *Maid of Lorn*

Class J37 0-6-0

64540	64579	64601	64628	64639
64541	64580	64611	64632	
64558	64581	64622	64633	
64578	64583	64623	64638	

Class J36 0-6-0

65221	65270	65296
65228	65273	65308

Class C15 4-4-2T

67456	67460	67467

Class C16 4-4-2T

67482	67485	67488	67500	67501

Class V1 2-6-2T

67600	67603	67644
67602	67618	67680

Class Y9 0-4-0ST

68103	68109	68118	68124

Class J88 0-6-0T

68326	68330	68336	68349
68327	68333	68347	

Class J83 0-6-0T

68447	68475	68479
68468	68476	68480

Class J69 0-6-0T

68551	68552

Class J72 0-6-0T

68709	69733

Class J50 0-6-0T

68953	68955	68957
68954	68956	68958

Class N14 0-6-2T

69120	69124

Class N15 0-6-2T

69126	69165	69178	69183	69203
69127	69166	69179	69184	69205
69131	69170	69180	69188	69208
69138	69176	69181	69189	69222
69163	69177	69182	69191	

Class Q1 0-8-0T

69925	69927

Class WD 2-8-0

90020	90174	90222	90313
90147	90192	90265	90441
90149	90193	90298	90545

Total 164

Allocations: 1959

Class 4 2-6-0

43135	43136	43137

Class 5 4-6-0

44702	44787	44956	44967	44970
44707	44908	44957	44968	44996

Class B1 4-6-0

61140	61197

61243 *Sir Harold Mitchell*

61261	61340	61342	61355	61396

Class K2 2-6-0
61764 *Loch Arkaig*

61785	61786

61787 *Loch Quoich*
61788 *Loch Rannoch*
61789 *Loch Laidon*
61794 *Loch Oich*

Class K4 2-6-0
61993 *Loch Long*
61994 *The Great Marquess*
61995 *Cameron of Lochiel*
61996 *Lord of the Isles*
61998 *MacLeod of MacLeod*

Class D34 4-4-0
62472 *Glen Nevis*
62474 *Glen Croe*
62477 *Glen Dochart*
62496 *Glen Loy*

Class D11 4-4-0
62671 *Bailie MacWheeble*
62672 *Baron of Bradwardine*
62673 *Evan Dhu*
62674 *Flora MacIvor*
62675 *Colonel Gardiner*
62676 *Jonathan Oldbuck*
62680 *Lucy Ashton*
62681 *Captain Craigengelt*
62682 *Haystoun of Bucklaw*
62684 *Wizard of the Moor*
62686 *The Fiery Cross*
62687 *Lord James of Douglas*
62689 *Maid of Lorn*

Class J37 0-6-0

64540	64558	64581	64623	64638
64541	64578	64611	64632	64639
64548	64580	64622	64633	

Class J36 0-6-0 No 65228 guards the southern entrance to No 14 road at Eastfield in 1958.
K. Fairey

Class J36 0-6-0
65228   65296   65315

Class C15 4-4-2T
67460   67474

Class C16 4-4-2T
67485

Classes V1 & V3 2-6-2T*
67600*   67603   67664   67671
67602   67644*   67667*   67680

Class J88 0-6-0T
68345   68352

Class J83 0-6-0T
68447   68468   68479

Class J50 0-6-0T
68952   68954   68955   68956   68957

Class N15 0-6-2T
69131   69171   69181   69188   69212
69163   69178   69182   69191   69214
69170   69179   69183   69197   69218

Class 5 4-6-0
73077   73078   73105   73108   73109

Class 4 2-6-0
76074

Class WD 2-8-0
90049   90489

Total 111

Allocations: 1965

Class B1 4-6-0
61008 *Kudu*
61116   61140   61342

Class 5MT 4-6-0
73078   73108

Total 6

Eastfield's last engines went to 66B Motherwell in November 1966.

65B ST ROLLOX

Pre-Grouping Origin: Caledonian Railway
Gazetteer Ref: 44 D4
Closed: 1966
Shed-Codes: 31A (1948 to 1949)
65B (1949 to 1966)
Allocations: 1950

Class 4P 4-4-0
40918   41126   41128

Class 5MT 2-6-0
42746

Class 4F 0-6-0
43848   44234   44256
43849   44255   44281

Class 5MT 4-6-0
44702   44881   44957   44996
44703   44922   44967   45115
44786   44923   44970   45116
44880   44956   44995   45153
45154 *Lanarkshire Yeomanry*
45155
45156 *Ayrshire Yeomanry*
45157 *The Glasgow Highlander*
45158 *Glasgow Yeomanry*
45159   45355   45443   45480   45499
45177   45356   45468   45481
45178   45423   45471   45482

Class 3P 4-4-0
54474   54475

Class 2P 0-4-4T
55121   55204

Looking west to St Rollox shed in 1949.   A. G. Ellis

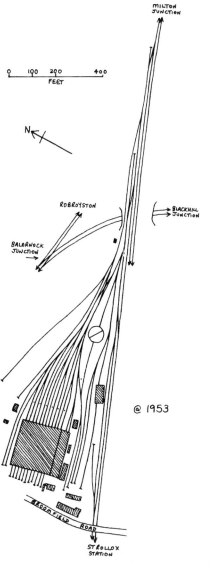

@ 1953

St Rollox shed roof was renewed in BR days as will be seen in this 1960 view of the depot. K. Fairey

Class 2F 0-6-0T
56151

Class 3F 0-6-0T
56233	56289	56330
56252	56310	56370

Class 2F 0-6-0
57240	57261	57318	57411	57454
57251	57269	57350	57434	57455
57253	57311	57352	57453	57457

Class 3F 0-6-0
57554	57558	57631
57557	57617	57686

Total 76

Allocations: 1959

Class 4 2-6-4T
42206   42207

Class 4 2-6-0
43140

Class 4F 0-6-0
44194   44199

Class 5 4-6-0
44677	44880	44922	45115	45153
44786	44881	44923	45119	

45157 *The Glasgow Highlander*
45158 *Glasgow Yeomanry*
45159	45355	45443	45482
45177	45356	45468	45499
45178	45358	45471	

Class 3P 4-4-0
54474   54475   54483   54501

Class 2F 0-6-0T
56151   56169

Class 3F 0-6-0T
56289   56370

Class 2F 0-6-0
57240	57258	57311	57411
57251	57261	57350	57426
57253	57269	57373	57434

Looking north across the running lines toward St Rollox shed in 1963, with a line of locos occupying the coaling road. Left to right are Classes 5MT 4-6-0 No 73152 (65B), 4MT 2-6-4T No 42269 (65A) and 5MT 4-6-0 No 45158 Glasgow Yeomanry *(65B).* S. Rickard

Class 3F 0-6-0

57557	57558	57617	57631	57686

Class D11 4-4-0
62688 *Ellen Douglas*

Class J88 0-6-0T
68349

Class 5 4-6-0

73145	73147	73149	73151	73153
73146	73148	73150	73152	73154

Class 4 2-6-0

76102	76103	76113	76114

Total 68

Allocations: 1965

Class 5MT 4-6-0

44718	45499

Class A4 4-6-2
60031 *Golden Plover*

Class 5MT 4-6-0

73145	73147	73149	73151	73153
73146	73148	73150	73152	73154

Total 13

An interesting feature of the 1950 figures is the allocation of all four named 'Black Fives'. St Rollox (formerly called Balornock) closed to steam in November 1966 when the last few locos transferred to 65J Stirling.

65C PARKHEAD

Pre-Grouping Origin: North British Railway
Gazetteer Ref: 44 D3
Closed: 1965 (see footnote)
Shed-Code: 65C (1949 to 1965)
Allocations: 1950

The western end of Parkhead depot in 1948 showing the original roof. J. L. Stevenson

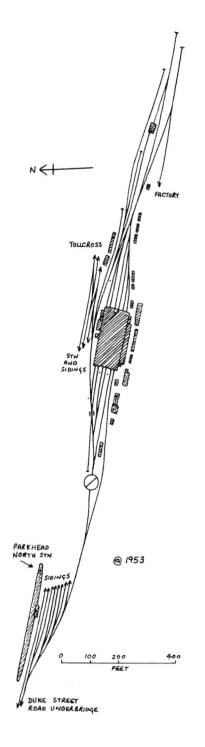

N ←

FACTORY

TOLLCROSS

STN
AND
SIDINGS

PARKHEAD
NORTH STN

SIDINGS

@ 1953

0   100   200   400
          FEET

DUKE STREET
ROAD UNDERBRIDGE

Class 5MT 4-6-0
44791

Class K2 2-6-0
61772 Loch Lochy

Class J37 0-6-0
64548   64563   64584   64610   64626
64559   64573   64609   64621

Class J36 0-6-0
65274   65283   65298   65324   65335

Class C15 4-4-2T
67454   67470   67479   67480

Class C16 4-4-2T
67487

Class V1 2-6-2T
67604   67621   67628   67655   67678
67611   67622   67633   67661   67681
67612   67623   67643   67662
67619   67626   67648   67676

Class J69 0-6-0T
68503   68567

Class N15 0-6-2T
69143   69171   69195   69210   69217
69151   69190   69198   69212
69157   69193   69199   69213
69161   69194   69209   69214

Class N2 0-6-2T
69500   69510   69514   69562   69565
69507   69511   69553   69564   69595

Total 68

Allocations: 1959

Class B1 4-6-0
61067   61117   61333   61344   61404

Class K2 2-6-0
61769
61772 Loch Lochy

Class J35 0-6-0
64461   64514   64520

Class J37 0-6-0
64559   64573   64609   64626
64563   64584   64621

Class J36 0-6-0
65211   65273   65295

Class C16 4-4-2T
67482   67487   67500

Parkhead's eastern entrance in 1961 with rebuilt roof in evidence. The Ivatt Class 4 2-6-0 facing is No 43136 and was one of five allocated to the depot at this time.   Real Photos

Classes V1 & V3* 2-6-2T

67607*	67623	67643*	67662*	67681*
67608	67626*	67648*	67675*	
67611*	67629	67650*	67676	
67612*	67630	67655	67678*	
67621	67633	67661	67679*	

Class J72 0-6-0T
69015

Class N15 0-6-2T

69161	69166	69194	69199	69213
69165	69190	69198	69209	

Class N2 0-6-2T

69507	69508	69509	69563

Total 58

Allocations: 1965

Ex-GNSR 4-4-0
49 *Gordon Highlander*

Ex-HR 4-6-0
103

Ex-CR 4-2-2
123

Ex-NBR 4-4-0
256 *Glen Douglas*

Total 4

Parkhead's regular allocation was gradually reduced in 1962 until the last few locos transferred to 65A Eastfield and 65F Grangemouth in January 1963. The shed was then considered a sub of Eastfield and continued with engines on loan. In October 1964 the four preserved engines (Nos 49, 103, 123 and 256) from ex-Scottish companies were allocated to Parkhead and were utilised on 'specials' throughout the Region. Final closure came in October 1965 and the veterans were moved to Kipps (65E).

65D DAWSHOLM

Pre-Grouping Origin: Caledonian Railway
Gazetteer Ref: 29 C5
Closed: 1964
Shed-Codes: 31E (1948 to 1949)
65D (1949 to 1964)
Allocations: 1950

Class 3MT 2-6-2T

40152	40158	40185	40188
40153	40176	40186	40189
40154	40177	40187	

Class 2P 0-4-4T
55168

Class 0F 0-4-0ST
56029

Class 2F 0-6-0T
56169   56171

Class 3F 0-6-0T
56302   56344

Class 2F 0-6-0

57245	57306	57341	57394	57470
57258	57314	57346	57426	57472
57273	57322	57372	57429	
57296	57336	57373	57456	

Dawsholm shed in 1948 depicting the remains of the original roof. The light from within would suggest the virtual non-existence of cover beyond the entrance. The depot was rebuilt in 1949. J. L. Stevenson

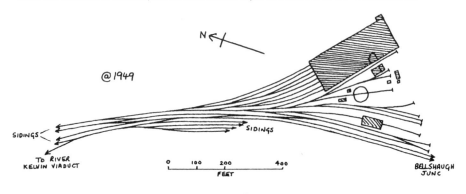

N

@ 1949

SIDINGS

SIDINGS

TO RIVER
KELVIN VIADUCT

0   100   200   400
FEET

BELSHAUGH
JUNC

Class 3F 0-6-0
57592   57605   57607   57612   57652

Class WD 2-8-0
90440   90549

Total 42

A 1958 view of the rebuilt Dawsholm with WD 2-8-0s dominating the scene. Real Photos

Allocations: 1959

Class 3 2-6-2T
40152	40158	40177	40188
40153	40159	40186	40189
40154	40176	40187	40200

Class 4 2-6-4T
42694

Class OF 0-4-0ST
56029

Class 2F 0-6-0T
56171

Class 3F 0-6-0T
56336

Class 2F 0-6-0
57245	57296	57336	57429	57472
57273	57314	57341	57470	

Class 3F 0-6-0
57554	57605	57612
57592	57607	57652

Class Y9 0-4-0ST
68114

Class J88 0-6-0T
68344

Class N15 0-6-2T
69126	69177	69205	69217
69176	69184	69208	

Class N2 0-6-2T
69511	69553

Class 4 2-6-0
76100	76101

Class WD 2-8-0
90114	90193	90436	90440	90493

Total 49

At closure in October 1964 the bulk of the remaining engines went to 65F Grangemouth and 66A Polmadie. Dawsholm played host to the four ex-Scottish preserved engines (see 65C) prior to their transfer to Parkhead.

65E KIPPS

Pre-Grouping Origin: NBR
Gazetteer Ref: 30 C5
Closed: 1963
Shed-Code: 65E (1949 to 1963)
Allocations: 1950

Class J35 0-6-0
64460	64472	64498	64531
64470	64473	64507	64534

Kipps from the east in 1961. The locos either side of the water tank are Classes V1 2-6-2T No 67623 of 67B (left) and J36 0-6-0 No 65216 Byng (65E). These latter locos, where named, usually had the name painted on the side of the middle splasher, although occasionally this adornment was omitted by paint-shop staff. Real Photos

Class J36 0-6-0
65210	65214
65217 French	
65226 Haig*	
65236 Horne	
65238	65249	65260	65266	65287
65245	65255	65264	65285	65325

*This loco was withdrawn in April 1951 and 65311 of the same class had acquired the name *Haig* by 1955.

Class C15 4-4-2T
67475

Class V1 2-6-2T
67627	67660	67665	67674

Class Y9 0-4-0ST No 68114 (65E) at the western end of Kipps in 1960 whilst sporting a wooden tender (see 65E notes). W. Potter

Class Y9 0-4-0ST

68094	68116	68120
68106	68117	68121

Class J88 0-6-0T

68329	68331	68343	68344

Class J83 0-6-0T

68442	68443	68444	68445	68461

Class N15 0-6-2T

69145	69196	69206	69207

Class N2 0-6-2T

69503	69509	69563
69508	69518	69596

Allocations: 1959

Class 4 2-6-0

43132	43133	43134

Class 2F 0-6-0T
56172

Class J35 0-6-0

64460	64472	64498	64531
64470	64473	64507	64534

Class J37 0-6-0

64574	64579	64628

Class J36 0-6-0

65210	65214

65217 *French*

65249	65266	65287	65343
65260	65285	65325	

Total 53

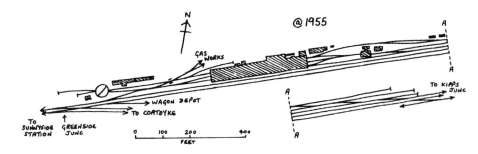

@ 1955

N

GAS WORKS

WAGON DEPOT

TO COATDYKE

To SUNNYSIDE STATION

GREENSIDE JUNC

TO KIPPS JUNC

A

A

A

A

0   100   200   400
FEET

66

Classes V1 * and V3 2-6-2T
67605   67618   67660   67674
67609   67627   67665*

Class Y9 0-4-0ST
68100*   68108*   68110   68117*   68123

Those locos marked * were known to have operated with makeshift wooden tenders (see photograph).

Class J88 0-6-0T
68336   68343

Class J83 0-6-0T
68442   68443   68444   68445

Class J72 0-6-0T
68709   68733

The Western end of Kipps shed in 1958 with Classes J36 0-6-0 No 65214 and J83 0-6-0T No 68444 (both 65E). Photomatic

Class N15 0-6-2T
69145   69196   69206   69207

Class N2 0-6-2T
69518   69596

Total 51

Whilst the bulk of Kipps' allocation went for scrap in December 1962, the last two engines (Nos 64593 & 65325), went to 65F Grangemouth and 65B St Rollox respectively in January 1963. The depot acted as a storage site for a number of years after closure.

65F GRANGEMOUTH

Pre-Grouping Origin: Caledonian Railway
Gazetteer Ref: 30 B4
Closed: 1965
Shed-Codes: 31D (1948 to 1949)
65F (1949 to 1965)
Allocations: 1950

Class 5MT 2-6-0
42736   42737

Class 4F 0-6-0
43883   44320

Class 3P 4-4-0
54483

Class 2P 0-4-4T
55119   55238

Class 2F 0-6-0T
56152   56164

Class 3F 0-6-0T
56230   56267   56300   56375
56243   56275   56336   56376

Grangemouth shed and coal stage in 1952.
A. G. Ellis

Allocations: 1959

Class 6P5F 2-6-0
42736   42737   42780   42802   42803

Class 4F 0-6-0
44234   44320

Class 2F 0-6-0
57265   57287   57338
57285   57334   57366

Class 2P 0-4-4T
55204   55214   55238

Class 3F 0-6-0
57667   57689   57691

Class 3F 0-6-0T
56376

Class WD 2-8-0
90134   90219   90236   90536   90616

Class 2F 0-6-0
57265   57285   57287   57338   57366

Class WD 2-10-0
90755   90757   90759   90765

Class 3F 0-6-0
57691

Total 35

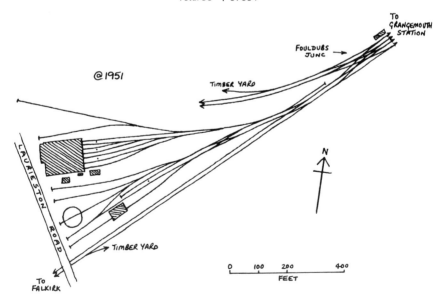

@ 1951

TO
GRANGEMOUTH
STATION

FOULDUBS
JUNC

TIMBER YARD

N

LAURIESTON ROAD

TIMBER YARD

TO
FALKIRK

0   100   200   400
FEET

Class J37 0-6-0
64588   64589   64592   64593

Class J36 0-6-0
65241   65246

Class J88 0-6-0T
68326

Class WD 2-10-0
90755   90759   90766
90757   90765   90769
90773 North British
90774
                              Total 32

Allocations: 1965

Class 5MT 4-6-0
44788   45177   45319   45443
44970   45192   45362   45488

Class 2MT 2-6-0
46460   46468

A westerley view of Grangemouth in 1954 with class
2P 0-4-4T No 55238 (65F) on the left and
Classes 4F, 3F and 2F 0-6-0 respectively, sharing
the right hand road.   Photomatic

Class J37 0-6-0
64580   64592   64610   64621

Class 5MT 4-6-0
73007   73105

Class 4MT 2-6-0
76045   76100   76102   76113
76046   76101   76103

Class 3MT 2-6-0
77006   77009

Class WD 2-8-0
90199   90489   90553   90560   90600
                                          Total 30

The bulk of Grangemouth's allocation was shared
between six other depots in October 1965, but the
last five engines transferred to 62C Dunfermline a
month later.

65G YOKER

Pre-Grouping Origin: Caledonian Railway
Gazetteer Ref: 29 C4
Closed: 1961
Shed-Code: 65G (1949 to 1961)

The turntable and coaling stage at Yoker a month
before closure in 1961. The shed is visible beyond
the coaler.   J. L. Stevenson

Allocations: 1950

Class OF 0-4-0ST
56030   56039

Class 2F 0-6-0T
56158   56161   56168   56170

Yoker MPD in 1958 with its solitary Class 2F 0-6-0 No 57259 at rest outside. Photomatic

Class 3F 0-6-0T
56238   56250   56297   56315   56339

Class 2F 0-6-0
57259

Class Y9 0-4-0ST
68112

Total 13

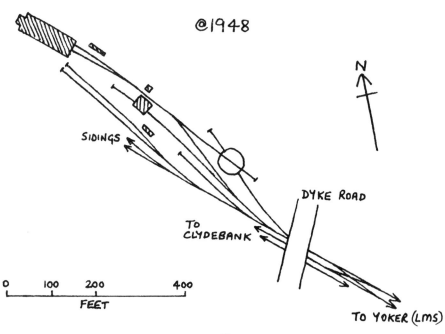

@1948

SIDINGS

N

DYKE ROAD

TO CLYDEBANK

TO YOKER (LMS)

0   100   200   400
FEET

70

Allocations: 1959

Class OF 0-4-0ST
56039

Class 2F 0-6-0T
56168

A pair of Class 3F 0-6-0Ts Nos 56250 (65G) and 56344 (65D) outside Yoker in 1952.
H. C. Casserley

Class 2F 0-6-0
57259

Total 3

Upon closure in March 1961 the locos were transferred to 65D Dawsholm.

65H HELENSBURGH

Pre-Grouping Origin: NBR
Gazetteer Ref: 29 B3
Closed: 1962
Shed Code: 65H (1949 to 1962)

Helensburgh shed in 1960 with Class V1 2-6-2T No 67602 (65A) outside. J. L. Stevenson

Allocations: 1950

Class V1 2-6-2T

67613	67616	67631
67614	67625	67632

Total 6

This 1954 view of Helensburgh shows (left to right) Classes V1 2-6-2T No 67613 (65H) and V3 2-6-2T No 67679 (65C) awaiting their duties. The former loco is bearing a '65C' shed plate thus illustrating the comment in the 65H notes. Real Photos

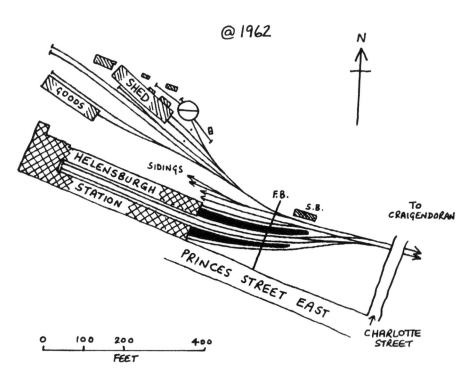

@ 1962

N

Two Class V3 2-6-2Ts Nos 67604 and 67632 (both 65H) await their next turns of duty outside Helensburgh shed in 1959. Note that the engine on the left is displaying a 'Bridgeton Central' destination sign over one of its buffers.   K. R. Pirt

Allocations: 1959

Class J37 0-6-0
64610

Class J36 0-6-0
65335

Classes V1 and V3 2-6-2T*
67604*	67614*	67619*	67625*	67631
67613	67616	67622	67628*	67632*

Total 12

The 1950 allocation is somewhat misleading as the depot also operated a number of 65C listed locos 'on loan' during that period. This situation was a product of Helenburgh's one-time existence as a sub-shed to 65C Parkhead. This parental control was never really shrugged, as it was reported in the late 1950s that many engines officially allocated to 65H were displaying 65C shed-plates. (See 1954 photograph.)

Ear-marked for closure in November 1960 as a result of the electrification of the area, Helensburgh enjoyed a stay of execution because of teething troubles with the change-over. It finally closed in December 1962 when the last loco departed for 65F Grangemouth. The shed was reported as being roofless in May 1961.

65I BALLOCH

Pre-Grouping Origin: NBR
Gazetteer Ref: 29 B3
Closed: 1961
Shed-Codes: 65J (1949 to 1950)
65I (1950 to 1961)
Allocations: 1950 (65I)

Class J36 0-6-0
65227	65315	65339

Class V1 2-6-2T
67601

Total 4

Allocations: 1959

Class J36 0-6-0
65339

Class V1 2-6-2T
67601

Total 2

As with Helensburgh, Balloch shed was due to close in November 1960 because of the electrification programme, and in fact, did so for a short while. It was hastily re-opened when the start of the new system was marred by voltage problems. The depot thus survived until mid-1961 when its last engine, No 67601, moved to 65A Eastfield.

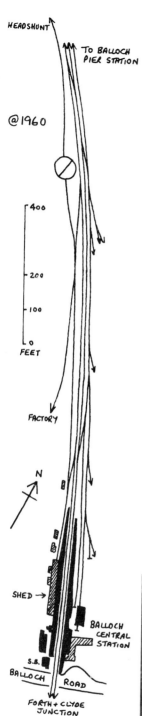

HEADSHUNT

TO BALLOCH
PIER STATION

@1960

⌀

400

200

100

0
FEET

FACTORY

N

SHED →

BALLOCH
CENTRAL
STATION

S.B.
BALLOCH ROAD

FORTH + CLYDE
JUNCTION

*Balloch 'shed' in 1950 devoid of locos. Balloch
Central station is on the left of the picture.*
J. L. Stevenson

The corrugated structure was erected circa-1948
and was the only means of shelter at the depot. It is
likely that its provision was due to Balloch being
afforded coded status within the motive power
network.

It was reported that on 31 May 1950, the
following were 'on shed': Nos (6)5227, 65315,
(6)5339 and 67601. All were carrying 65I shed-
plates but, as will be seen from the numbers, two
were still in LNER livery. These four engines
comprised the total 1950 allocation of the depot.

*Class J36 0-6-0 LNER No 9280 at Balloch in 1946
prior to the erection of the corrugated structure.*
J. L. Stevenson

66A POLMADIE

Pre-Grouping Origin: Caledonian Railway
Gazetteer Ref: 44 E3
Closed: 1967
Shed-Codes: 27A (1948 to 1949)
66A (1949 to 1967)
Allocations: 1950

Class 4P 4-4-0
40916   41131

Class 4MT 2-6-4T

42167	42203	42238	42247	42692
42168	42204	42239	42274	42693
42169	42205	42240	42275	42694
42170	42206	42241	42276	42695
42171	42207	42242	42277	42696
42172	42213	42243	42688	42698
42200	42214	42244	42689	42699
42201	42215	42245	42690	
42202	42216	42246	42691	

Class 4F 0-6-0
44196

Class 5MT 4-6-0

44707	44790	44793	45484	45486
44787	44792	44794	45485	45487

'Jubilee' 4-6-0
45579 *Punjab*
45583 *Assam*
45584 *North West Frontier*
45691 *Orion*
45692 *Cyclops*

'Royal Scot' 4-6-0
46102 *Black Watch*
46104 *Scottish Borderer*
46105 *Cameron Highlander*
46107 *Argyll and Sutherland Highlander*
46121 *Highland Light Infantry, City of Glasgow
      Regiment*

'Coronation' 4-6-2
46220 *Coronation*
46221 *Queen Elizabeth*
46222 *Queen Mary*
46223 *Princess Alice*
46224 *Princess Alexandra*
46227 *Duchess of Devonshire*
46230 *Duchess of Buccleuch*
46231 *Duchess of Atholl*
46232 *Duchess of Montrose*

Class 3F 0-6-0T

47331	47536	47540
47332	47537	47541

Class 2P 0-4-4T

55141	55179	55207	55265
55167	55197	55224	55267
55170	55201	55228	55268

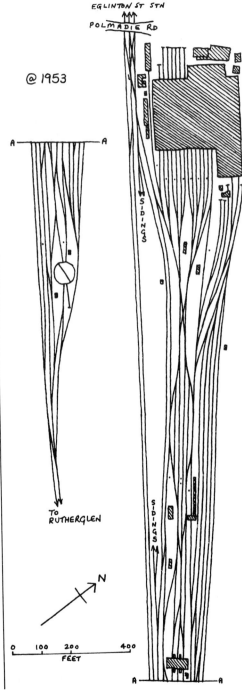

@ 1953

75

Looking north-west to Polmadie from the scissors crossing in 1948.   J. L. Stevenson

Class 2F 0-6-0T

56153	56159	56162
56154	56160	56167

Class 3F 0-6-0T

56239	56280	56298	56308	56342
56244	56281	56304	56314	56346
56260	56292	56305	56318	56349
56261	56294	56306	56322	
56263	56295	56307	56324	

Class 2F 0-6-0

57230	57292	57361	57412	57447
57238	57317	57365	57432	57448
57239	57319	57367	57433	57459
57268	57320	57370	57439	57463
57271	57321	57387	57443	57464
57275	57347	57388	57444	57465
57288	57360	57389	57446	

Class 3F 0-6-0

57555	57581	57622	57630	57674
57564	57619	57625	57661	57690

Total 166

Allocations: 1959

Class 4 2-6-4T

42055	42060	42172	42245	42276
42056	42143	42239	42246	42277
42057	42144	42242	42268	42695
42058	42170	42243	42274	
42059	42171	42244	42275	

Class 4F 0-6-0

43848	44193	44256	44318
43849	44251	44283	44322

'Royal Scot' 4-6-0
46102 *Black Watch*
46104 *Scottish Borderer*
46105 *Cameron Highlander*
46107 *Aryll and Sutherland Highlander*
46121 *Highland Light Infantry, City of Glasgow Regiment*

'Princess' 4-6-2
46201 *Princess Elizabeth*
46210 *Lady Patricia*

Polmadie shed in 1961. In the centre three unidentified 'Coronation' Pacifics can be seen (two facing).   W. T. Stubbs

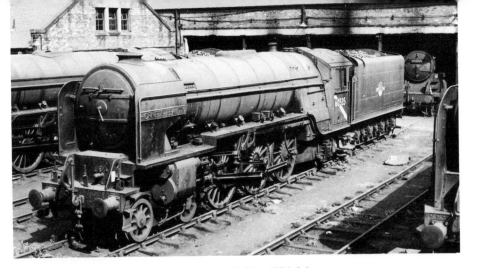

In 1965 Polmadie possessed three of the remaining six Class A2 4-6-2's. Here we see one of these No 60535 Hornets Beauty *at the western end of the shed in 1965.* G. W. Sharpe

'Coronation' 4-6-2
46222 *Queen Mary*
46223 *Princess Alice*
46224 *Princess Alexandra*
46227 *Duchess of Devonshire*
46230 *Duchess of Buccleuch*
46231 *Duchess of Atholl*
46232 *Duchess of Montrose*

Class 3F 0-6-0T
47536   47541

Class 8F 2-8-0
48773   48774   48775

Class 2P 0-4-4T
55167	55201	55224	55239
55169	55207	55228	55265
55189	55223	55237	55268

Class 2F 0-6-0T
56153	56154	56158	56159	56160

Class 3F 0-6-0T
56239	56266	56298	56318	56335
56241	56292	56304	56322	56349
56260	56295	56308	56324	

Class 2F 0-6-0
57239	57292	57361	57417	57448
57268	57317	57365	57418	57463
57271	57319	57367	57419	57465
57275	57347	57369	57432	
57288	57360	57389	57444	

Class 3F 0-6-0
57553	57563	57581	57622	57674
57555	57564	57603	57625	

Class J35 0-6-0
64471   64477   64511

Class J36   0-6-0
65216 *Byng*
65232

Class J50 0-6-0T
68953   68958

'Britannia' 4-6-2
70050 *Firth of Clyde*
70051 *Firth of Forth*
70052 *Firth of Tay*

'Clan' 4-6-2
72000 *Clan Buchanan*
72001 *Clan Cameron*
72002 *Clan Campbell*
72003 *Clan Fraser*
72004 *Clan Macdonald*

Class 5 4-6-0
73055	73058	73061	73064	73076
73056	73059	73062	73072	73098
73057	73060	73063	73075	73099

Class 3 2-6-0
77008   77009

Class 4 2-6-4T
80001	80007	80027	80057	80108
80002	80022	80054	80058	80110
80003	80023	80055	80106	80129
80006	80026	80056	80107	80130

Class WD 2-8-0
90039	90134	90229	90387	90596
90060	90198	90234	90536	90616
90077	90199	90320	90549	90640

Class WD 2-10-0
90751   90767

Total 182

A brace of Class 4MT 2-6-4Ts outside Polmadie in 1966. Left is No 80027 (66A) whilst on the right No 80122 (66D) replenishes its tanks.   C. Lofthus

Allocations: 1965

Class 4MT 2-6-4T

42131	42199	42277
42195	42243	42690

Class 5MT 4-6-0

44721	44796

Class A2 4-6-2
60512 *Steady Aim*
60522 *Straight Deal*
60535 *Hornet's Beauty*

Class 5MT 4-6-0

73055	73060	73063	73072	73098
73059	73062	73064	73075	73099

Class 4MT 2-6-0

76004	76070	76071

Class 4MT 2-6-4T

80001	80057	80108	80116	80121
80002	80058	80109	80118	80123
80027	80086	80110	80120	80130
				Total 39

Surviving right up to the end of steam traction on the Scottish Region on 1 May 1967, Polmadie's 12 remaining locos were withdrawn.

66B MOTHERWELL

Pre-Grouping Origin: Caledonian Railway
Gazetteer Ref: 30 C5
Closed: 1967
Shed-Codes: 28A (1948 to 1949)
66B (1949 to 1967)

The southern end of Motherwell MPD in 1959.
W. T. Stubbs

Allocations: 1950

Class 3MT 2-6-2T
40159   40200

Class 4MT 2-6-4T
42125   42126   42127   42208

Class 4F 0-6-0
43884

Class 5MT 4-6-0
44969   45009   45151   45176   45498
45008   45121   45152   45462

Class 3P 4-4-0
54441   54460   54464
54453   54462   54465

Class 4MT 4-6-0
54630   54635   54640   54648   54650
54634   54636   54647   54649   54654

Class 2P 0-4-4T
55134   55138   55188   55191

Class 2F 0-6-0T
56155   56172

Class 3F 0-6-0T
56241   56264   56271   56334   56345
56245   56265   56276   56335   56356
56247   56268   56277   56337   56357
56258   56269   56285   56338   56358

Class 2F 0-6-0
57247   57289   57328   57404   57435
57256   57291   57332   57414   57436
57267   57299   57335   57416   57437
57270   57303   57363   57417   57461
57272   57325   57377   57418   57462
57278   57326   57379   57419

Class 3F 0-6-0
57582   57593   57599   57659   57688
57588   57595   57638   57666   57681

Class WD 2-8-0
90044   90152   90585   90693
90125   90386   90628

Class WD 2-10-0
90750   90756   90761   90770
90752   90758   90762   90771
90754   90760   90766   90772

Total 116

Allocations: 1959

Class 4 2-6-4T
42125   42127   42203   42689   42699
42126   42200   42208   42696

Class 4F 0-6-0
43883   43884

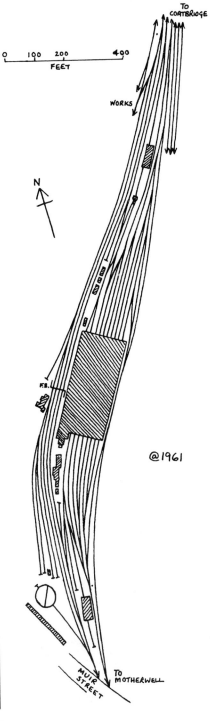

79

Another view of Motherwell from the south, this time in 1951. Note the difference in track geometry with the 1959 view. H. I. Cameron

Class 5 4-6-0

44850	45029	45151	45433	45498
44969	45085	45152	45462	
45008	45099	45176	45484	
45009	45121	45309	45485	

Class 3P 4-4-0

54462	54464	54465

Class 3F 0-6-0T

56264	56285	56338	56367
56269	56337	56356	

Class 2F 0-6-0

57237	57270	57303	57363	57435
57247	57278	57325	57377	57436
57256	57291	57326	57404	57461
57267	57299	57328	57414	57462

Class 3F 0-6-0

57593	57599	57659	57668	57688
57595	57638	57666	57681	

Class 4 2-6-0

76000	76002	76004	76071
76001	76003	76070	

Class 2 2-6-0

78050	78051

Class WD 2-8-0

90071	90386	90468	90628

Class WD 2-10-0

90750	90754	90758	90761	90770
90752	90756	90760	90762	

Total 89

Allocations: 1965

Class 5MT 4-6-0

44786	44850	44908	45029	45498
44787	44880	44991	45176	
44820	44881	45009	45433	

Class 2MT 2-6-0

46463

Class 5MT 4-6-0

73107

Class 4MT 2-6-0

76000	76002	76003

Class 3MT 2-6-0

77005	77008

Total 20

Surviving as it did until the end of steam traction on the Scottish Region, Motherwell's last seven locos were withdrawn in May 1967.

One of Motherwells Black Five allocation No 45029 outside the South entrance to the shed in 1955. Photomatic

66C HAMILTON

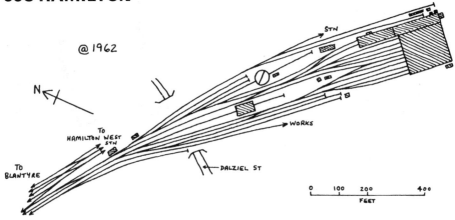

@ 1962

N ←

TO STN

↗ STN

→ WORKS

TO
HAMILTON WEST
STN

TO
BLANTYRE

DALZIEL ST

0	100	200		400

FEET

Pre-Grouping Origin: Caledonian Railway
Gazetteer Ref: 44 B2
Closed: 1962
Shed-Codes: 27C (1948 to 1949)
66C (1949 to 1962)
Allocations: 1950

Class 3MT 2-6-2T
40150   40151

Class 4MT 2-6-4T
42128   42130   42165
42129   42164   42166

Class 5MT 2-6-0
42735   42740   42741   42850   42880

Class 4MT 2-6-0
54638   54639

*Hamilton shed in 1959 with the following members
of its allocation present, Nos 42128, 44196 and
42850. It was reported that by 1960 four lanes had
been given up for DMU maintenance.*
J. L. Stevenson

Class 2P 0-4-4T
55146   55221

Class 3F 0-6-0T
56237   56284   56303   56321
56242   56286   56309   56360
56255   56287   56319   56362
56256   56296   56320   56371

Class 2F 0-6-0
57237   57250   57307   57398   57413
57242   57260   57384   57407   57430
57244   57280   57395   57410   57431

Class 3F 0-6-0
57609   57663   57665

Total 51

Allocations: 1959

Class 4 2-6-4T
42128   42164   42166
42129   42165   42167

Class 6P5F 2-6-0
42735   42738   42746   42850   42880

Hamilton a decade earlier with Classes 2F 0-6-0 No 57430 and 5MT 2-6-0 No 42740 (both 66C) simmering outside.   H. C. Casserley

Class 4F 0-6-0
44196

Class 3F 0-6-0T
47331

Class 3F 0-6-0T

56242	56286	56296	56321	56362
56256	56287	56309	56360	56371

Class 2F 0-6-0

57242	57307	57370	57407	57447
57244	57321	57384	57431	
57250	57335	57398	57446	

Class 3F 0-6-0

57609	57630	57663	57665

Class 3 2-6-0

77005	77006	77007

Class 4 2-6-4T
80109

Class WD 2-10-0

90764	90771	90772

Total 47

Hamilton's last few serviceable engines were transferred to 66B Motherwell and 66A Polmadie in December 1962.

66D GREENOCK LADYBURN

Pre-Grouping Origin: Caledonian Railway
Gazetteer Ref: 29 B3
Closed: 1966
Shed-Codes: 27B (1948 to 1949)
66D (1949 to 1966)
Allocations: 1950

Class 4P 4-4-0

41148	41149	41182

Class 4MT 2-6-4T

42175	42415	42418	42421	42697
42176	42416	42419	42422	
42400	42417	42420	42423	

Class 2F 0-6-0T

47167	47168	47169

Class 3P 4-4-0

54440	54468	54492	54498	54508
54457	54479	54497	54506	

Class 0F 0-4-0ST

56028	56031	56035

Class 2F 0-6-0T

56156	56163	56166
56157	56165	56173

The eastern end of Greenock Ladyburn in 1954 prior to rebuilding as a five road depot. Note the three 'Caley Pugs' (Class OF 0-4-0ST) in a row near the centre. Photomatic

Class 3F 0-6-0T
56288

Class 2F 0-6-0
57369

Class 3F 0-6-0
57552   57556   57682

Total 42

@ 1965

To
CARTSDYKE STN

To
BOGSTON
STN
SID

B

N

0   100   200   400

FEET

Allocations: 1959

Class 4 2-6-4T

42175	42241	42260	42263	42266
42176	42258	42261	42264	42698
42236	42259	42262	42265	

Class 6P5F 2-6-0

42740	42741

Class 4F 0-6-0
44011

Class 2F 0-6-0T

47167	47168	47169

Class 3P 4-4-0

54468	54479	54497	54498	54506

Class 2P 0-4-4T
55267

Class OF 0-4-0ST

56031	56035

Class 2F 0-6-0T

56163	56166	56170
56165	56167	56173

Class 2F 0-6-0
57416

Class 3F 0-6-0

57552	57619	57682	57690

Total 39

The rebuilt Ladyburn in 1963 from the north-west. J. L. Stevenson

Allocations: 1965

Class 4MT 2-6-4T

42170	42216	42260	42266
42176	42241	42264	42694
42197	42259	42265	

Class 4MT 2-6-4T
80060

Total 12

Greenock closed in December 1966 when its last engine (No 80122) was withdrawn from service.

67A CORKERHILL

Pre-Grouping Origin: GSWR
Gazetteer Ref: 44 E3
Closed: 1967
Shed-Codes: 30A (1948 to 1949)
67A (1949 to 1967)
Allocations: 1950

Class 2P 4-4-0

40594	40598	40620	40636	40642
40595	40599	40621	40637	40649
40596	40604	40627	40641	40651

Class 4P 4-4-0

40905	40909	40915
40906	40914	40919

Class 4MT 2-6-4T

42122	42190	42193	42196
42123	42191	42194	42197
42124	42192	42195	

Class 5MT 2-6-0

42911	42914	42916	42917

Class 4F 0-6-0

43899	44159	44198	44329

Class 5MT 4-6-0

44706	45049	45174	45489
44968	45163	45194	45490
45047	45168	45251	45491

'Jubilee' 4-6-0
45560 *Prince Edward Island*
45576 *Bombay*
45643 *Rodney*
45645 *Collingwood*
45646 *Napier*
45693 *Agamemnon*

Class 3F 0-6-0T
47329

Class 2P 0-4-4T

55135	55182	55219	55266
55140	55206	55225	55269
55143	55211	55235	

Class 3F 0-6-0T

56249	56329	56350	56361	56369

Class 2F 0-6-0

57241	57255	57300	57359
57249	57266	57309	

Class 3F 0-6-0

57560	57566	57580	57596	57698
57562	57575	57589	57695	

Total 91

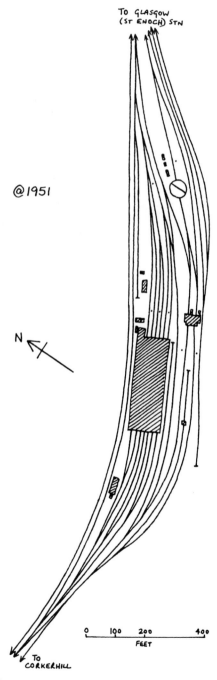

A 1962 view of Corkerhill from the western approaches. W. T. Stubbs

Allocations: 1959

Class 2P 4-4-0

40594	40599	40627	40641
40596	40620	40636	40642
40598	40631	40637	40639

Class 4 2-6-4T

42122	42190	42193	42238	42247
42123	42191	42229	42240	

Class 4F 0-6-0

43899	44001	44198
43996	44189	44319

Class 5 4-6-0

44706	45007	45161	45251	45489
44791	45160	45194	45362	45490

'Jubilee' 4-6-0

45621 Northern Rhodesia
45665 Lord Rutherford of Nelson
45677 Beatty
45687 Neptune
45693 Agamemnon
45707 Valiant
45711 Courageous
45720 Indomitable

Class 3F 0-6-0T
47329

Class 2P 0-4-4T

55206	55219	55225	55235	55266

Class 2F 0-6-0T
56156

Class 3F 0-6-0T

56279	56361	56364

Class 2F 0-6-0

57241	57249	57300	57359

Class 5 4-6-0

73079	73101	73103	73121	73123
73100	73102	73104	73122	73124

Class 4 2-6-0

76090	76092	76094	76096	76098
76091	76093	76095	76097	76099

Class 4 2-6-4T

80000	80009	80025	80127
80008	80024	80030	80128

Total 87

Allocations: 1965

Class 5MT 4-6-0

44791	44798	45171

Class 5MT 4-6-0

73005	73079	73102	73106	73122
73009	73100	73103	73120	73123
73057	73101	73104	73121	73124

Class 4MT 2-6-0

76093	76114

Class 2MT 2-6-0

78026

Class 4MT 2-6-4T

80000	80024	80047	80112
80004	80025	80051	80128
80020	80046	80063	

Total 32

Corkerhill survived until the end of steam traction on the Scottish Region in May 1967, when its last three locos were withdrawn.

Looking north to the western end of Corkerhill in 1954 with (left to right) Classes 4P 4-4-0 No 41133, 3F 0-6-0T No 56350 and 4P 4-4-0 No 41142 (all 67A). Photomatic

A view of Corkerhill's eastern approaches from the coaling tower in 1948. J. L. Stevenson

67B HURLFORD

Pre-Grouping Origin: GSWR
Gazetteer Ref: 29 E4
Closed: 1966
Shed-Codes: 30B (1948 to 1949)
67B (1949 to 1966)

Hurlford shed in 1950. J. L. Stevenson

Allocations: 1950

Class 2P 4-4-0

40566	40593	40618	40661	40686
40570	40597	40619	40662	40687
40571	40605	40643	40663	40688
40572	40612	40644	40665	40689
40573	40617	40645	40666	

Class 4P 4-4-0
41110

Class 5MT 2-6-0
42744   42745   42910   42912

Class 4F 0-6-0
44312   44319   44323   44325

Class 3P 4-4-0
54456   54504

Class 2P 0-4-4T
55203   55236   55260

Class 3F 0-6-0T
56236   56368

Class 2F 0-6-0
57236   57277   57331   57353   57383

Class 3F 0-6-0
57570   57573   57650   57672
57571   57637   57651   57688
57572   57643   57671

                                    Total 56

Allocations: 1959

Class 3 2-6-2T
40049

Class 2P 4-4-0
40570   40593   40612   40661   40689
40571   40597   40619   40665
40572   40605   40643   40686
40573   40608   40644   40687
40592   40609   40645   40688

Class 6P5F 2-6-0
42743   42744

Class 4F 0-6-0
44281   44312   44325

Class 5 4-6-0
45010   45266

Class 2P 0-4-4T
55203   55211   55264

Class 3F 0-6-0T
56368

Class 2F 0-6-0
57236   57295   57353
57284   57331   57383

Class 3F 0-6-0
57562   57577   57650   57672
57570   57637   57651   57689
57572   57643   57671

Class 3 2-6-0
77015   77016   77017   77018   77019
                                    Total 55

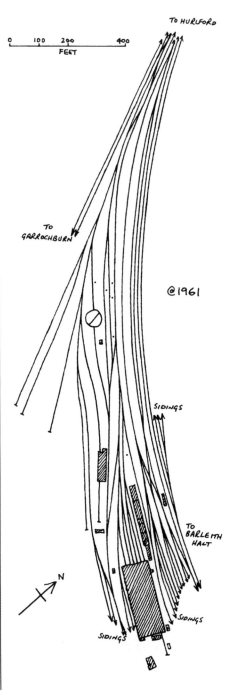

89

The coaling stage at Hurlford and shed beyond in 1953. B. Hilton

Allocations: 1965

Class 5MT 2-6-0
42736	42739	42741	42795	42879

Class 5MT 4-6-0
44955	44992	45124	45490
44972	45117	45489	

Class 2MT 2-6-0
46451

Class 4MT 2-6-0
76021	76091	76094
76024	76092	76108

Class 3MT 2-6-0
77007	77016	77018
77015	77017	77019

Class 4MT 2-6-4T
80029	80091	80111

Total 28

Closing in December 1966, Hurlford's last engine (45124) was transferred to 67A Corkerhill.

67C AYR

Pre-Grouping Origin: GSWR
Gazetteer Ref: 29 F3
Closed: 1966
Shed-Codes: 30D (1948 to 1949)
67C (1949 to 1966)
Allocations: 1950

Class 2P 4-4-0
40574	40590	40638	40647	40664
40575	40610	40640	40648	40670

Class 4P 4-4-0
40908	41132	41138	41183
40920	41133	41155	

Class 4MT 2-6-4T
42131

Class 5MT 2-6-0
42739	42806	42809	42927
42805	42808	42879	

'Sentinel' 0-4-0T
47182

Class 2P 0-4-4T
55132	55240	55262	55264

Class 3F 0-6-0T
56257	56273	56363
56272	56274	56367

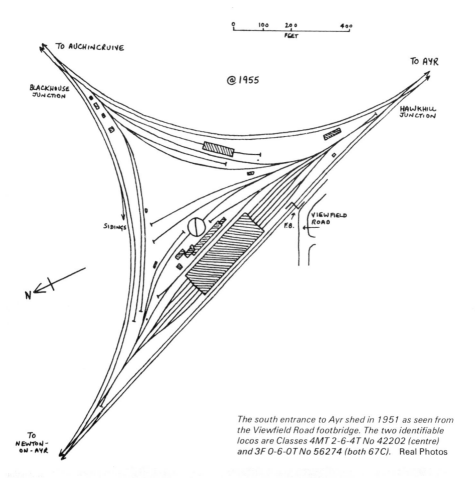

@1955

TO AUCHINCRUIVE

BLACKHOUSE JUNCTION

TO AYR

HAWKHILL JUNCTION

SIDINGS

VIEWFIELD ROAD

F.B.

N

To NEWTON-ON-AYR

0   100   200   400
FEET

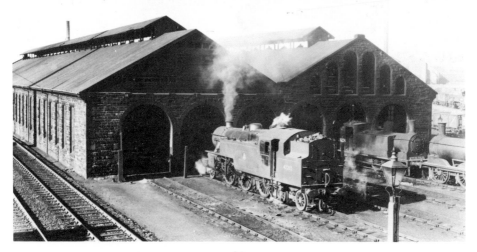

The south entrance to Ayr shed in 1951 as seen from the Viewfield Road footbridge. The two identifiable locos are Classes 4MT 2-6-4T No 42202 (centre) and 3F 0-6-0T No 56274 (both 67C). Real Photos

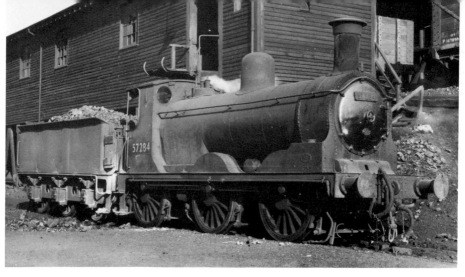

Class 2F 0-6-0 No 57284 (67C) alongside the coaling stage at Ayr in 1951. Real Photos

Class 2F 0-6-0

57234	57279	57312	57364
57235	57284	57315	57392
57262	57295	57354	

Class 3F 0-6-0

57569	57614	57633	57658
57594	57615	57640	57684
57611	57628	57644	57697

Total 59

Allocations: 1959

Class 2P 4-4-0

40574	40590	40610	40647	40670
40575	40595	40640	40664	

Class 4 2-6-4T

42131	42195	42197	42202
42194	42196	42201	

Class 6P5F 2-6-0

42739	42808	42910	42917
42745	42809	42914	42927
42805	42879	42916	

Class 4F 0-6-0

44323	44329	44330	44331

Class 2P 0-4-4T

55231	55262

Class 3F 0-6-0T

56252	56344	56363	56372

Class 2F 0-6-0

57262	57279	57354	57364	57392

Class 3F 0-6-0

57569	57611	57628	57644
57580	57614	57633	57658
57596	57615	57640	57684

Class Y9 0-4-0ST

68124

Class WD 2-8-0

90319	90463	90505

Total 58

The northern end of Ayr shed in 1957. Left to right are Black Five 4-6-0 No 45121 (66B) and '4MT' 2-6-4Ts Nos 80030 and 80009 (both 67A). The Newton-on-Ayr to Ayr running lines occupy the foreground. G. W. Morrison

Allocations: 1965

Class 5MT 2-6-0

42702	42789	42861	42912	42919
42737	42800	42863	42913	
42740	42801	42908	42916	
42780	42803	42909	42917	

Class 5MT 4-6-0

44974	45160	45164	45365	45486
44977	45161	45167	45460	

Class 2MT 2-6-0

46413	46482	46498

Class 4MT 2-6-0

76001	76096	76098

Total 32

Ayr's last two locomotives, namely Nos 76096 and 76101 were withdrawn in December 1966.

67D ARDROSSAN

Pre-Grouping Origin: GSWR
Gazetteer Ref: 29 D3
Closed: 1965
Shed-Codes: 30C (1948 to 1949)
67D (1949 to 1965)
Allocations: 1950

Class 2P 4-4-0

40578	40607	40624	40667
40579	40608	40625	40668
40606	40609	40626	40669

Class 4MT 2-6-4T

42209	42210	42211	42212

Class 3F 0-6-0T

56259	56279	56282	56311	56364

Class 2F 0-6-0

57263	57276	57348	57356
57274	57282	57355	57357

Class 3F 0-6-0

57577	57590	57669
57579	57627	57673

Total 35

Allocations: 1959

Class 2P 4-4-0

40578	40607	40626	40667
40579	40624	40638	40668
40606	40625	40666	40669

Class 4 2-6-4T

42124	42210	42212
42209	42211	42697

Class 6P5F 2-6-0

42742	42806	42911	42912

Class 4F 0-6-0

44159

Class 5 4-6-0

45456	45457

The south-eastern end of Ardrossan shed in 1954 with Classes 2P 4-4-0 No 40609 (left) and 5MT 2-6-0 No 42742 (both 67D) on display.
Photomatic

A selection of six-coupled stock outside Ardrossan in 1946. Note the positioning of the shed-plates on each of the three locos smokebox doors. Despite their usual placement on the bottom, the practice of fixing these castings to the top of the doors was not uncommon at certain Scottish Section sheds of the LMSR.   J. L. Stevenson

Class 3F 0-6-0T
56259   56352

Class 2F 0-6-0
57254   57266   57309   57355   57357
57263   57274   57348   57356

Class 3F 0-6-0
57566   57590   57669
57579   57627   57673

Total 42

At closure in February 1965, the remaining engines were transferred to 67C Ayr.

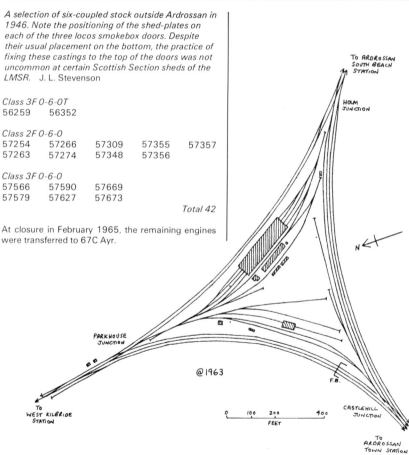

TO ARDROSSAN
SOUTH BEACH
STATION

HOLM
JUNCTION

N

PARKHOUSE
JUNCTION

@1963

F.B.

TO
WEST KILBRIDE
STATION

CASTLEHILL
JUNCTION

0   100   200   400
FEET

TO
ARDROSSAN
TOWN STATION

68A KINGMOOR

Pre-Grouping Origin: Caledonian Railway
Gazetteer Ref: 26 C1
Closed: 1968
Shed-Codes: 12A (1948 to 1949)
68A (1949 to 1958)
12A (1958 to 1968)
Allocations: 1950 (68A)

Class 2P 4-4-0

40602	40613	40615

Class 4P 4-4-0

41129	41140	41142	41146
41139	41141	41143	

Class 5MT 2-6-0

42720	42780	42833	42876	42899
42748	42793	42834	42877	42905
42749	42802	42835	42881	42906
42751	42803	42836	42882	42907
42752	42831	42837	42883	42913
42757	42832	42875	42884	

Class 4F 0-6-0

43868	43996	44016	44199
43902	44001	44181	44315
43922	44008	44183	44324
43973	44009	44189	44326

Class 5MT 4-6-0

44668	44677	44726	44898	45082
44669	44718	44727	44899	45083
44670	44719	44795	44900	45084
44671	44720	44877	44901	45100
44672	44721	44878	44902	45126
44673	44722	44882	44903	45363
44674	44723	44883	44993	45364
44675	44724	44884	44994	45432
44676	44725	44886	45081	45455

Kingmoor (south) in August 1961 with two 'Coronation' 4-6-2's in the distance. Nearer the camera are two Class 3F 0-6-0s Nos 43622 (left) and 57653 (both 12A) languishing on the scrap road. The former ex-Midland, the latter ex-Caledonian, they were withdrawn from stock in December 1959 and January 1961 respectively. W. Potter

'Jubilee' 4-6-0

45577 *Bengal*
45580 *Burma*
45581 *Bihar and Orissa*
45582 *Central Provinces*
45713 *Renown*
45714 *Revenge*
45715 *Invincible*
45716 *Swiftsure*
45727 *Inflexible*
45728 *Defiance*
45729 *Furious*
45730 *Ocean*
45731 *Perseverance*
45732 *Sanspareil*

Class 8F 2-8-0

48321	48464	48472	48536	48612

Class 3F 0-6-0T

56231	56266	56327	56340	56373
56235	56316	56332	56354	56374
56248	56317	56333	56355	

Class 3F 0-6-0

57632

Class WD 2-8-0

90464	90505

Class WD 2-10-0

90751	90767	90773
90763	90769	90774

Total 142

Allocations: 1959 (12A)

Class 2P 4-4-0

40602	40613	40615	40651

Class 4 2-6-4T

42440	42542

Class 6P5F 2-6-0

42720	42804	42835	42881	42906
42748	42830	42836	42882	42907
42751	42831	42837	42883	
42752	42832	42875	42884	
42757	42833	42876	42899	
42793	42834	42877	42905	

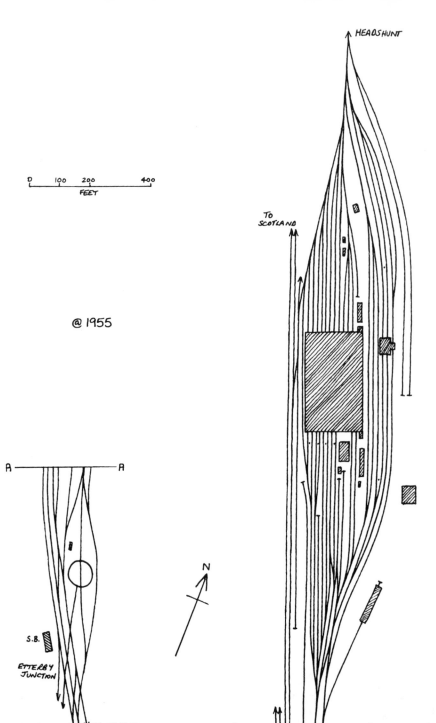

HEADSHUNT

TO
SCOTLAND

@ 1955

0   100   200   400
         FEET

A ——————— A

N

S.B.

ETTERBY
JUNCTION

TO CARLISLE

A ——————— A

Class 3F 0-6-0
43241	43514	43622	43678

Class 4F 0-6-0
43902	44008	44181	44315
43922	44009	44183	44324

Class 5 4-6-0
44668	44726	44886	45013	45138
44669	44727	44898	45018	45163
44670	44790	44899	45081	45330
44671	44792	44900	45082	45334
44672	44795	44901	45083	45363
44673	44877	44902	45100	45364
44674	44878	44903	45118	45455
44675	44882	44958	45120	45466
44676	44883	44993	45122	45481
44725	44884	45012	45126	45491

'Jubilee' 4-6-0
45640 Frobisher
45657 Tyrwhitt
45679 Armada
45691 Orion
45696 Arethusa
45697 Achilles
45704 Leviathan
45713 Renown
45714 Revenge
45715 Invincible
45716 Swiftsure
45718 Dreadnought
45724 Warspite
45728 Defiance
45729 Furious
45730 Ocean
45731 Perseverance
45732 Sanspareil

Class 3F 0-6-0T
47332	47515	47537	47667
47358	47527	47540	

The northern end of Kingmoor in 1963 with (left to right) Classes 5MT 4-6-0 (named), 'Clan' 4-6-2 and A3 4-6-2. N. E. Preedy

Class 8F 2-8-0
48321	48474	48612	48756
48464	48536	48708	48758

Class 3F 0-6-0T
56235	56332	56340	56374
56316	56333	56373	

Class 3F 0-6-0
57653

'Clan' 4-6-2
72005 Clan Macgregor
72006 Clan Mackenzie
72007 Clan Mackintosh
72008 Clan MacLeod
72009 Clan Stewart

Class WD 2-8-0
90170	90464

Class WD 2-10-0
90763

Total 143

Allocations: 1965 (12A)

Class 4MT 2-6-0
43000	43023	43040	43139
43004	43028	43049	

Class 4F 0-6-0
43981	44451

Class 5MT 4-6-0
44668	44792	44903	45118	45254
44669	44795	44986	45120	45259
44670	44802	44993	45126	45293
44671	44878	45012	45135	45295
44672	44883	45013	45138	45363
44674	44884	45018	45148	45364
44677	44886	45028	45163	45442
44689	44887	45061	45185	45455
44692	44898	45082	45195	45481
44726	44899	45097	45217	45491
44727	44900	45105	45228	
44767	44901	45106	45235	
44790	44902	45112	45236	

An earlier view of the southerly entrance to
Kingmoor in 1954. Left of centre is 'Clan' 4-6-2
No 72008 Clan Macleod (68A).   Photomatic

'Patriot' 4-6-0
45530 Sir Frank Ree
45531 Sir Frederick Harrison

'Jubilee' 4-6-0
45574 India
45588 Kashmir
45629 Straits Settlements
45742 Connaught

'Royal Scot' 4-6-0
46115 Scots Guardsman
46128 The Lovat Scouts
46140 The King's Royal Rifle Corps
46160 Queen Victoria's Rifleman

Class 3F 0-6-0T
47326   47471   47641   47667

'Britannia' 4-6-2
70001 Lord Hurcomb
70002 Geoffrey Chaucer
70003 John Bunyan
70005 John Milton
70006 Robert Burns
70007 Coeur-de-Lion
70008 Black Prince
70009 Alfred the Great
70016 Ariel
70035 Rudyard Kipling
70036 Boadicea
70037 Hereward the Wake
70038 Robin Hood
70039 Sir Christopher Wren
70040 Clive of India
70041 Sir John Moore

Carlisle Kingmoor interior with Black Five 4-6-0's
Nos 44706 and 45082 in the centre of the view.
Note the manner in which the smoke troughs are
suspended from the roof supports.   Ian Allan Library

'Clan' 4-6-2
72005 *Clan Macgregor*
72006 *Clan Mackenzie*
72007 *Clan Mackintosh*
72008 *Clan MacLeod*
72009 *Clan Stewart*

Class 9F 2-10-0

92009	92015	92021	92076	92233
92010	92017	92023	92130	
92012	92019	92024	92208	

Total 119

As will be seen from the shed-codes, Kingmoor was London Midland Region property from 1958 until its demise in January 1968 when most of the allocation was withdrawn from service. A small number of locos found homes at South Lancashire sheds for the few months that remained of the 'steam era'.

An interesting feature of the 1965 listings is the inclusion of five different named classes despite the 50% plus proportion of 'Black Fives' and the high rate of dieselisation at that time. Also worth noting is that all five of the 'Clan' engines which survived into this year were Kingmoor based and had been since 1958. The class became extinct in May 1966 with the withdrawal of No 72006 from 12A Kingmoor.

68D DUMFRIES

Pre-Grouping Origin: GSWR
Gazetteer Ref: 26 B3
Closed: 1966
Shed-Codes: 12G (1948 to 1949)
68B (1949 to 1962)
67E (1962 to 1966)
Allocations: 1950 (68B)

Class 3MT 2-6-2T
40170

Class 2P 4-4-0

40576	40577	40614

Class 4P 4-4-0

40902	40912	41135	41175
40904	41109	41171	41179

Class 5MT 2-6-0

42908	42909	42915	42918	42919

Class 3P 4-4-0

54443	54444	54507

Class 2P 0-4-4T

55124	55164

Class 2F 0-6-0

57302	57337	57349	57378	57397
57329	57344	57362	57391	57405

Class 3F 0-6-0

57563	57601	57621
57600	57602	57623

Total 38

Dumfries MPD in 1953 as seen from the Annan Road overbridge with Class 2P 4-4-0 No 40614 (68B) posing in the foreground. J. L. Stevenson

Allocations: 1959 (68B)

Class 3 2-6-2T
40151   40170

Class 2P 4-4-0
40576   40577   40614

Class 6P5F 2-6-0
42908   42913   42918
42909   42915   42919

Class 5 4-6-0
44995   45169   45432   45480

Class 3P 4-4-0
54502   54507

Class 2P 0-4-4T
55124   55232

Class 3F 0-6-0T
56310   56327

Class 2F 0-6-0
57302   57329   57349   57362   57378

An interior view of Dumfries in 1954.
J. L. Stevenson

Class 3F 0-6-0
57600   57601   57602   57621   57623

Class 4 2-6-0
76072   76073

Total 33

Allocations: 1965 (67E)

Class 5MT 4-6-0
44699   44723   45115   45463   45471
44707   44995   45432   45467   45480

Class 2MT 2-6-0
46450   46479

Class 4MT 2-6-0
76073   76074

Class 2MT 2-6-0
78051

Class 4MT 2-6-4T
80023   80061   80117   80119

Total 19

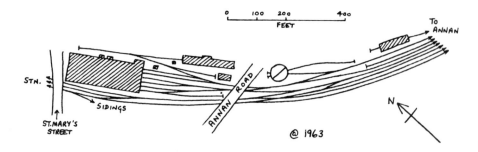

STN.

ST.MARY'S
STREET

SIDINGS

ANNAN ROAD

0   100   200   400
FEET

To
ANNAN

N

@ 1963

At closure in May 1966, the bulk of the remaining stock was transferred to 67A Corkerhill and 67B Hurlford.

Dumfries shed in 1934. The building was of the same design as its double-ended ex-GSWR sister shed at Ayr. W. Potter

68C STRANRAER

Pre-Grouping Origin: Caledonian & GSWR
Gazetteer Ref: 25 C2
Closed: 1966
Shed-Codes: 12H (1948 to 1949)
68C (1949 to 1962)
67F (1962 to 1966)
Allocations: 1950 (68C)

Class 2P 4-4-0
40600   40611   40616   40623

Class 4P 4-4-0
41092   41099   41127

Class 2P 0-4-4T
55125

Class 3F 0-6-0T
56234   56372

Class 2F 0-6-0
57375   57445   57458

Total 13

Allocations: 1959 (68C)

Class 2P 4-4-0
40566   40611   40616   40623

Class 6P5F 2-6-0
42749

Class 5 4-6-0
45125

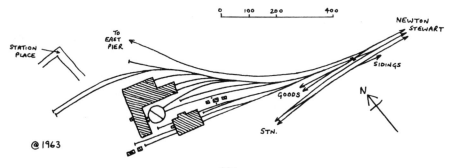

Class 3P 4-4-0
54492   54508

Class 2P 0-4-4T
55240

Class 3F 0-6-0T
56302

Class 2F 0-6-0
57238   57340   57375   57445

Class 4 2-6-0
76112

Total 15

The ex-GSWR shed at Stranraer in 1962 with visiting 'Clan' 4-6-2 No 72006 Clan Mackenzie (12A). This engine became the last survivor of its class and was withdrawn in May 1966. Note the rebuilt shed entrances compared with the original archways on the right of the view. K. Fairey

An overall view of Stranraer depot in 1954. The rebuilt ex-Caledonian structure is on the left whilst the ex-Glasgow & South Western building can be seen beyond the right of the coaling plant.
J. L. Stevenson

Allocations: 1965 (67F)

Class 5MT 4-6-0
44999

Class 4MT 2-6-0
76112

Class 2MT 2-6-0
78016

Total 3

Stranraer lost its last engine (45463) to 67C Ayr in October 1966.

The depot consisted of two buildings, one of Caledonian origin, the other Glasgow and South

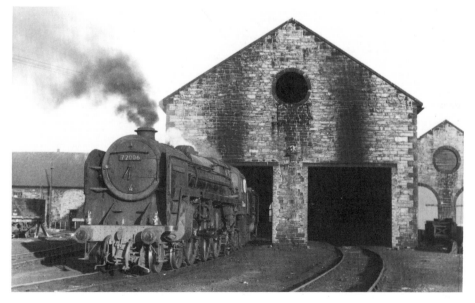

Western. In pre-grouping days these two companies together with the LNWR and Midland comprised the Portpatrick & Wigtownshire Joint line which served the area.

The ex-Caledonian shed at Stranraer in 1962.
K. Fairey

68D BEATTOCK

Pre-Grouping Origin: Caledonian Railway
Gazetteer Ref: 30 G3
Closed: 1967
Shed-Codes: 12F (1948 to 1949)
68D (1949 to 1962)
66F (1962 to 1967)
Allocations: 1950 (68D)

Class 1P 2-4-2T
46656

Class 2P 0-4-4T
55142   55181   55232   55234   55239

The northern end of Beattock shed in 1949 with the station visible on the far left. J. L. Stevenson

55178	55220	55233	55237

Class 4P 4-6-2T

55350	55353	55360
55352	55359	55361

Total 16

Allocations: 1959 (68D)

Class 4 2-6-4T

42130	42205	42214	42688
42192	42213	42215	

Class 2P 0-4-4T

55234	55260

Class 3F 0-6-0
57568

Total 10

Allocations: 1965 (66F)

Class 4 2-6-4T
42129   42688   42693

Class 4MT 2-6-0
76090

Class 4MT 2-6-4T
80005   80045

Total 6

Surviving as it did until the end of steam on the Scottish Region in May 1967, Beattock's last two locos went for scrap.

Beattock shed as viewed from the station with a pair of Class 2P 0-4-4Ts Nos 55164 and 55260 (both 68D). T. Wright

The depot's main role was the provision of banking engines for the gruelling Northward climb to Beattock Summit. In 1950 the shed boasted all the surviving ex-Caledonian 4P 4-6-2Ts. Twelve were built in 1917 and all except two survived nationalisation. The class became extinct in October 1953 when No 55359 was withdrawn (from 68D) (see accompanying photograph).

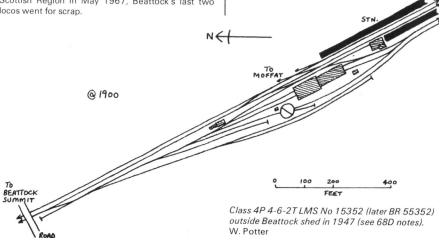

@ 1900

Class 4P 4-6-2T LMS No 15352 (later BR 55352) outside Beattock shed in 1947 (see 68D notes). W. Potter

List of Shed-Codes

The following lists sets out every shed-code that existed for steam Motive Power Depots under the Scottish Region from 1949 to 1967 along with each venue and its length of occupancy.

60A	Inverness	1949-62
60B	Aviemore	1949-62
60C	Helmsdale	1949-62
60D	Wick	1949-62
60E	Forres	1949-59
61A	Kittybrewester	1949-61
61B	Ferryhill	1949-67
61C	Keith	1949-61
62A	Thornton	1949-67
62B	Dundee Tay Bridge	1949-67
62C	Dunfermline	1949-67
63A	Perth	1949-67
63B	Stirling South	1949-60
	Fort William	1960-62
63C	Forfar	1949-58
	Oban	1959-62
63D	Fort William	1949-55
	Oban	1955-59
63E	Oban	1949-55
64A	St Margarets	1949-67
64B	Haymarket	1949-63
64C	Dalry Road	1949-65
64D	Carstairs	1949-60
64E	Polmont	1949-60
64F	Bathgate	1949-66

64G	Hawick	1949-66
65A	Eastfield	1949-66
65B	St Rollox	1949-66
65C	Parkhead	1949-65
65D	Dawsholm	1949-64
65E	Kipps	1949-63
65F	Grangemouth	1949-65
65G	Yoker	1949-61
65H	Helensburgh	1949-62
65I	Balloch	1950-61
65J	Balloch	1949-50
	Fort William	1955-60
	Stirling South	1960-66
65K	Polmont	1960-64
66A	Polmadie	1949-67
66B	Motherwell	1949-67
66C	Hamilton	1949-67
66D	Greenock Ladyburn	1949-66
66E	Carstairs	1960-66
66F	Beattock	1962-67
67A	Corkerhill	1949-67
67B	Hurlford	1949-66
67C	Ayr	1949-66
67D	Ardrossan	1949-65
67E	Dumfries	1962-66
67F	Stranraer	1962-66
68A	Kingmoor	1949-58
68B	Dumfries	1949-62
68C	Stranraer	1949-62
68D	Beattock	1949-62
68E	Carlisle Canal	1951-58

That most saddening of sights — a redundant motive power depot. The remains of Wick in 1966 (closed 1962).   P. Foster

A line up of stored ex-Caledonian Class 3P 4-4-0s at
Greenock Princes Pier shed (sub of 66D) in 1956.
Left to right are Nos 54443, 54492, 54479 and
54506 (all 66D).   D. A. Anderson

Class B1 4-6-0 No 61278 (62B) rests outside
Aberdeen Ferryhill on 3 March 1967 after hauling
the 19.45 freight from Dundee. As the predominance
of diesel power suggests, Ferryhill closed to steam in
this month.   D. Mackinnon

A quaint but effective method of coaling at some
small sheds was the hoist and bucket system
illustrated here. When suspended over the locos
bunker the side door would be unlatched to allow
gravity to do the rest. The one shown is at Alloa (sub
of 62C) in 1966.   P. R. Parham

A stark contrast to the hoist and bucket system is this view of Dundee Tay Bridge mechanical coaling plant in 1964. Shed Pilot Class J36 0-6-0 No 65319 (62B) is also depicted sporting a cab-tender.
M. Pope

Class B1 4-6-0 No 61278 (62B) again (see Ferryhill night view), this time at St Margarets shed in 1965. D. R. Easton

The south-west corner of Corkerhill shed in 1966 clearly depicting the predominance of BR Standard classes. The notice relates to the compulsory stabling of locos clear of the crossing.   C. Lofthus

The idyllic setting of Kyle of Lochalsh (sub of 60A) in 1957 with a trio of Black Five 4-6-0s (left to right) Nos 44783, 45478 and 44719 (all 60A). Also 'on shed' at this time were Nos 45192, 45476 and Class 2P 0-4-4T No 55216 (all 60A).   A. W. Martin

Index